How 1000s of Childcare Centers and Schools Are Making Millions

Make your early education company more effective, less stressful, more profitable and more valuable.

Brad Barnett
President of BFS®

Brad is the ultimate professional in his work with childcare facilities.
- Edward Flegal, Senior Credit Officer at Live Oak Bank

I first got involved with Brad in 2003 when he engaged NovaCopy to provide document solutions to BFS®. I was immediately impressed with his business acumen and communication skills. Since that time, Brad has become a trusted advisor to me and a friend. Brad has an impeccable reputation. I highly recommend Brad to anyone for important business dealings where the highest levels of trust and expertise are required.
- Darren Metz, CEO, NovaCopy

Dedicated, knowledgeable and trustworthy, Brad works tirelessly for his clients. As an expert in his field, his knowledge is unsurpassed, but it is his integrity that I most admire.
- Chalayne Sayes, CEO, MBC Media

Owning Rainbow Kids for nearly 16 years and being faced with foreclosure, the options of selling it were extremely limited. It was just sheer luck that I had seen the postcard about BFS®. I quickly learned how thorough and knowledgeable they were about the entire process. I had some experience with selling property. Given this prior experience, I became even more impressed with my primary point of contact being with Brad Barnett who is the President and Broker for BFS® (Barnett Real Estate Services, Inc.). BFS® helped me turn the center around. Over the many years and hundreds of transactions they have perfected the business of facilitating the sale of childcare centers and schools. Brad and his staff not only surpassed my expectations during the sale and assisted to resolve any of the inevitable issues which arise when dealing with attorneys, but...anytime I got worried as my bank's foreclosure date loomed, Brad stepped in to ensure the timeline was met and the deal was closed. I would have been relieved to simply sell my center and not have the penalties involved in foreclosing and having 22 staff members and 99 parents to explain why the center was shut down. My asking price was $1.2 million and I received $1,195,000…nobody except for BFS® could have achieved that level of success. I would highly recommend them…you will find their level of professionalism and expertise will help you to surpass any goals you have set.

- James Sullivan, President, Rainbow Kids Learning Center, Norton, MA

Brad Barnett has been a pleasure to work with due to an extremely high level of professionalism, communication, credibility, integrity and value. He not only treats each business partner and customer with a high level of service, but truly makes you feel valued. As an expert in his field with exceptional knowledge and competency, I would highly recommend Brad and BFS®.

- John Handmaker, CEO, Q2 Business Capital

We have been an innovator and leader in the childcare industry for the State of Ohio for 50 years. Our centers served close to 2000 children per day. We discussed and investigated the best approach to take with our bankers, business associates, investment advisors, and industry brokers. It did not take long for us to realize that Brad Barnett of BFS®/Barnett Real Estate Services, Inc. was the best person/organization to retain. His industry knowledge, practical philosophy, professional approach, and personal commitment proved to us that he would find the best match to sell our centers and continue our family legacy. Brad's approach was always upfront, honest, supportive, and we could count on him to deliver whatever he committed to do for us.

- Philip Wenk, Ph.D., MBA, President, Creative Playrooms, Inc.

As a fellow entrepreneur I have always been impressed with Brad's initiative and drive, but by far the most impressive element of my experience with Brad is his outstanding character. He is the type of ethical, above-board businessman we all hope to find sitting across the table in any sort of business dealing. I highly recommend him.
- Dan Hogan, Entrepreneur

I've known Brad for 32 years (since college). We have done business together and we've been friends since that time. I have always known him to do what he says he will do, and on the time frame he promises. From my experience he has demonstrated a trustworthiness that is indeed rare in today's business environment.
- Jeff Marzolf, President, Marzolf Investment Group, LLC

Selling a business can be a complex and arduous process that warrants the talents, expertise and knowledge of a professional. BFS® successfully and quickly procured a buyer and negotiated the sale, initiating frequent communication and providing the much needed advice and knowledge of an experienced broker. I would highly recommend BFS® to broker the acquisition and/or sale of a business without hesitation.
- Carole Revell, CEO, Learning Ladder Corp

I have had the opportunity to work with Brad and his company for over ten years. The relationship has been a pleasure, based on sound communication, trust and loyalty. Throughout that time, Brad has always proved to be the type of person you look forward to doing business with: sharp, to the point, honest, reasonable, and committed. I am confident that any endeavor one would undertake with Brad would result in success.
- Michael Spurgeon, President, Fidelity Offset, Inc.

After 23 years as owners of Kid's Castle Child Care Learning Center, in Brookfield, CT, my husband, Mike and I sold our center. We could not have done this without the help of Brad Barnett at BFS®. Our lease was expiring in 5 months, which is not an ideal situation for a buyer to enter. Yet, Brad was able to bring us together with someone willing to strike a good deal with our landlord. There were many obstacles along the way and Brad was there for me.
- Cathy DeFreitas, Owner/Director, Kid's Castle Child Care Learning Center, Brookfield, Ct

After talking with Brad Barnett off and on for years, we hired BFS® to represent us in the sale of our two childcare centers in Christiana and New Castle, Delaware. We met with Brad. He explained the process in detail…We were off and running, but there were many difficulties to navigate during the process. I doubt that most transactions are as difficult as ours, but every time it looked like we were at an impasse, BFS® found a way to make it work. They explain everything up front. They do genuinely professional work. They keep their word.
- Dan Frost, President, Panda Early Education Centers

Brad Barnett of BFS® was our broker for selling our business and property, a private school and childcare facility. We chose Brad because he not only had tremendous experience in selling schools and childcare businesses, it is his exclusive domain. Brad was very patient with us…We found him to be professional, organized and responsive. Brad, himself, is very personable, diplomatic and an effective communicator. These traits are important…We highly recommend Brad and BFS®.
- Laura Witmondt, Former President
- Richard Witmondt, Former Secretary/Treasurer
- Village Montessori School of Roswell, Inc. Roswell, GA

When my parents decided they were ready to sell their schools and retire, we wanted to be sure the process was managed professionally. Brad Barnett met with my parents Nan and Stu Howkins, our CPA, and me. He was honest and direct and provided us with realistic expectations we understood. The BFS® team was there for everything we needed in both transactions. They didn't just find buyers and sell the schools. They used their detailed knowledge of the market and our specific area to maximize the benefits to our family. You can really see their experience and professionalism in the way they are prepared for everything before it happens…these are the people that you want with you.

-Heidi Lockwood,

- Nan Howkins, President

- Stu Howkins, Secretary

- The Children's Corner, Inc.

- Kaleidoscope Kids, Inc.

Brad Barnett from BFS® impressed me from my first phone call with him to Brad getting on a plane and traveling over 800 miles to (discreetly) tour my childcare center. After the tour, Brad took the time to discuss and determine my goals. He did this with an extensive gathering of information. This provided him with the information he needed to understand and explain my childcare business to potential buyers. BFS® also created the correct marketing materials and the accurate pricing for my center. After working with Brad and his BFS® team, I can attest that seeking their services was the best choice for achieving my professional and personal goals. I had originally worked with another local M&A firm prior to BFS®. It was not a positive experience. Because of Brad's knowledgeable expertise, he was able to provide many qualified potential buyers, many making offers. I was fortunate enough to be able to choose which company I felt was the perfect match for my childcare company. If you're look-ing for a professional, experienced and dedicated group to help with your exit planning and beyond, BFS® will be the only call you need to make. Thank you for all you did from my first phone call.

- Mary Innocenzi, CEO, The Village Learning Center, Pennington, NJ

It has been quite a few years, but it seems that you and your firm haven't missed a beat. Congratulations! I want this email to serve as a strong endorsement of BFS®/Brad Barnett and recommendation to anyone seeking to purchase or sell preschool businesses anywhere in this country. My opinion is that BFS® is THE company to broker preschool businesses. The prompt results were due to you and your firm's expertise, efficient preparation of the offer to sell, and most importantly, your knowledge of our immediate market area, including active buyers and sellers. Personally, it was a pleasure to work with you.

- Ron Stephens, Former President, Teddy Bear Treehouse Preschools, Inc., San Diego, CA

I have to be honest that I was initially cynical about using your services. As you know, I have a background in finance; I have been in the industry for almost 25 years and I have worked in real estate. Add to that the fact that I have been on both sides of the fence, as a seller & a buyer innumerable times, without the services of a broker. I therefore questioned what your company could bring to the table that I was not already bringing. I am now a convert. What you & your company bring to the table is beyond my 'pay grade' & my Universe! I will never sell another center, without using your services. It was an unmitigated pleasure working with you & Lisa.

- Donny Banerji, President, A Child's World, Jamestown, NC

The most important aspect of selling the school for us was making sure the new owners would treat the children, parents and staff as family, the way we had done during our many years operating the school. Brad was able to understand this important element above and beyond his excellent ability in determining the value of the business and bringing qualified buyers to the table. He was there from start to finish…I would have to say that there is a reason for them being the largest in the nation.

\- Eric Alino, Vice President, Vinland & Associates, Inc.

As the recent past owner of Pleasant Day Schools, LLC (PDS) it is my pleasure to comment on the performance of Brad Barnett and his Barnett Financial Services (BFS®) team in acting as our broker for the sale of PDS. PDS, located in Morgantown, West Virginia, was the first childcare center in the state to achieve national accreditation by the NAEYC…from the first moment we met him we were impressed with his professional demeanor and very personal approach to learning about PDS. In summary, Brad and the BFS® team gave us tremendous service.

\- Art Tribbie, Pleasant Day Schools, Morgantown WV

We hired BFS® to sell our childcare company based on their track record of many successful childcare sales in New York as well as the rest of the country. It is with genuine confidence that I recommend their services. The process was simple, comprehensive and effective. We signed the agreement to hire them. Brad Barnett immediately flew to our location and discreetly evaluated our company. BFS® took our company to market, found the qualified buyer we needed, secured the necessary financing for the buyer and closed the transaction while allowing us to receive all cash at the closing. While our negotiation and sale was difficult, I felt as if BFS® had everything under control at all times. The people at BFS® could not have been nicer or more professional.

\- Robert Garcia, Former Owner, The Small Miracle Preschool Center, Ltd., Ossining, NY

We wanted to thank you for all of the help you gave us before, and during the selling of our childcare. We thank you for the personal touch. Brad, you were wonderful, and Katie and I really consider you a friend, as well as a fabulous business associate.
- Sandra Sokol and Katie Sasser, Former Owners of Franklin Childcare II, LLC, Franklin, TN

Thanks for the handling of the sale of Fletcher's Daycare Center. We appreciate all the extra attention and understanding which you gave us to make this happen. You made it clear that whatever we needed was most important. Everyone we caused to come in contact with you, from our staff, the buyers and our attorney, all stated that you are always very professional and efficient. This was also our experience throughout the process with your entire staff. We both feel that without BFS® this would not have been nearly as pleasant of an experience.
- Mr. Edward C. Fletcher, Former President
- Mrs. Ramona M. Fletcher, Former Vice President
- Fletcher's Inc., Quincy, IL

We felt that our center would be very hard to sell being that we were fairly new. We were amazed that it happened in a shorter time than we expected. Not only did you sell it for us, but also negotiated an exceptional price. You walked us through everything step-by-step. You performed above and beyond our expectations.
- Ms. Kimberly G. Pinckney, Former President MAAK, Inc., Kathleen, GA

A great big thank you for the handling of the first and second centers of Happy Day Care, Inc. I appreciate all of the extra attention, understanding and help that you gave me to make this happen. I am very pleased with the results both financially and in the way it was structured and implemented. It was especially nice to have you visit with Susan after the sale and help me celebrate. My family, which is of most importance to me, appreciates having met you and also thank you for the business relationship.

- Ms. Rosemarie "Ro" Day, Former President, Happy Day Care, Inc., East Syracuse and Manlius, NY

How 1000s of Childcare Centers and Schools Are Making Millions

Make your early education company more effective, less stressful, more profitable and more valuable.

Brad Barnett
President of BFS®

Brad Barnett
BFS®, Inc.
1321 Murfreesboro Road
Suite 501
Nashville, TN 37217
www.bfsinc.net

This publication is designed to provide competent information regarding the subject matter covered based on the experience of the author. However, it is sold with the understanding that the author and publisher are not engaged in tendering legal, financial, or other professional advice. Laws and practices vary from state to state and if legal or other professional assistance is required, the services of a professional licensed in the appropriate state should be sought. The author and publisher specifically disclaim any liability that is incurred from the use or application of the contents of this book.

Legal Disclaimer: Always consult with the proper professionals before taking action. By and before the use of this information provided herein, reader agrees that BFS® is not responsible for reader's actions related to said information and reader recognizes that no action should be taken solely on the basis of the information contained herein.

How 1000s of Childcare Centers and Schools Are Making Millions/Brad Barnett. 1st edition.
ISBN 978-1-7342705-0-1

CONTENTS

Introduction 1

SECTION 1 - MANAGING
Avoiding The Pitfalls

How Do I Manage Problem Employees In My Childcare Center? 7

How Should I Structure My Childcare and Its Real Estate? 15

Being Prepared For An Emergency In Early Education 17

How To Limit The Liability In My Montessori School (Or Childcare Center) 21

Avoiding Lawsuits In The Early Education Industry 25

Defending Your Profits

When Should I Raise Rates For My Montessori School (or Childcare Center)? 29

How Do I Fix Collection Problems In My Childcare Center? 31

Payroll and Your Montessori School or Childcare 37

How To Reduce or Control Expenses In Your Early Education Company 39

Designing Your Childcare or School Space 51

What Should I Expect When A New Childcare Center or School Opens Close To Me? 55

The State Is Cutting Our Subsidy. What Should I Do? 57

How Much Should My Major Expenses Be For My School or Childcare Center? 61

How To Handle A Minimum Wage Increase In The Early Education Industry 63

How To Hire Great Long-Term Staff For Your Early Education Company 65

How To Increase The After Tax Income Of Your Early Education Company 69

Know How To Count Your Money In Early Education......................71

More Money and Less Debt For Your Early Education Company 75

Best People. Best Centers.

Leadership In Your Childcare Center or School 79

Selecting The Right Team For Your Early Education Company 83

Building A Team For Your Childcare Company or School...............89

Montessori Teaching Growing Faster In U.S....................................91

What You Do Matters – Here's Some Proof......................................93

Winning Daily

Early Education – How To Have Productive Meetings 97

Dealing With Change In Your Childcare Company or School 101

The Importance of Communication In Your Childcare Company or School...105

Mother or Management – What Children and Schools Need...........107

SECTION 2 - GROWING
Using Tech To Grow

Using Twitter To Market Your Childcare Company........................111

Why You Need A Website For Your Childcare Company or School
....115

How Do I Use Social Media To Improve My Early Education Company?...117

Why Should I Take The Time To Create A Monthly Newsletter For My Childcare Center or School? 119

Using Video To Market Your Childcare Company, Preschool, Montessori School or Private Elementary 123

Using Pinterest To Improve Your Early Education Company 127

Embracing Technology In Your Early Education Company............129

Humans For Growth

Connecting With Parents In Your Early Education Company 133

Expanding Your Early Education Company 137

Promoting Your Teachers and Your School Through Curriculum and Confidence 141

How Do I Increase Enrollment In My Childcare Center or School? 145

Why Parents and Teachers Love Montessori 149

SECTION 3 - SELLING
Timing Your Sale

How Long Does It Take To Sell An Early Education Company? ... 153

Market Timing In The Early Education Industry 157

How Do I Know When It's Time To Sell My Early Education Company? 161

How To Get The Most

How To Get The Best Appraisal For Your Early Education Real Estate At The Best Price 165

Is My Multi-Unit Early Education Company Worth More If I Sell Multiple Centers Simultaneously? 167

Sale and Leaseback Transactions 173

What To Do With Used Furniture, Fixtures and Equipment (FF&E) 177

SECTION 4 - Buying
All About The Benjamins

Choosing The Right Bank 181

How Much Down Payment Money Do I Need To Buy An Early Education Company? 185

SBA Fees Explained 189

Should I Use Conventional or SBA Financing? 191

SBA Makes Money Easier With Lending Parameters 195

The Mechanics of Buying

Top Four Mistakes Buyers Make When Applying For Financing... 199

How High Does My Credit Score Need To Be And How Do I Make It Better? 203

What Information Should A Letter of Intent Include? 207

Funding Your Early Education Company 213

How Can I Get The Best Loan Terms For My Early Education
Company?...215

What Are The Initial Questions I Should Ask About An Early
Education Company If I'm Interested In Buying It?........................219

About BFS®...223

Summary of Services...225

About The Author...227

Introduction

Is it possible for a nothing-special, skinny little kid in a small childcare center in East Nashville, TN to fight a family history of poverty, mandatory drug rehabs, gun fights (yes, I said gun fights), limited education and plain bad luck to graduate college with honors and become a millionaire because he recognized the extreme importance of early education?...Of course it is. However, this is not a book about some guy who made a business decision and got rich. This is the culmination of two decades of focus and tenacity that started with the desperation of a child.

"How 1000s of Childcare Centers & Schools Are Making Millions" is the product formed from assisting/improving many thousands of early education companies throughout the U.S. during the last 25+ years and assembling that information in one place so current early education company executives, owners, directors, teachers and industry newcomers don't have to learn everything the hard way. Instead, you're holding the answers in your hand right now. It's like walking into a test and already having the answers…except you're not cheating.

When I discussed this book with my confidants, we discussed how to price it. I thought to myself that we could make it really inexpensive…basically, give it away. Then we discussed, what's it really worth? If you use a few of the ideas from the book and you increase your annual income by $100,000 a year, then assuming 10 years of use…10 years X $100,000…the price of the book should be $1,000,000. While the mathematics can support the higher price, we thought $1,000,000 was a little extreme. So, here you are with a $40 book in your hand. Is it a good investment? It is…if you use it.

Author Brad Barnett (former skinny little kid), founded BFS® in 1993 and currently serves as its President. BFS® is a consulting firm with a longstanding Better Business Bureau A+, references from early education professionals all over the U.S. and licensed professionals in 42 states and Washington DC. BFS® specializes solely in the early education vertical and has assisted thousands of early education companies (day care, childcare, preschools, Montessori and private elementary schools) with Management, Financing, Evaluations, Buying, Selling, Real Estate Transactions and more. Visit www.bfsinc.net for more information.

Brad understands the importance of engaging children in learning as soon as possible. A child that likes to learn, or at least learns how to learn, has an entirely different trajectory for his or her life. If you are a director, a teacher, an owner or executive in the early education industry, then you do have the power to change these lives.

1. Benefits and Highlights: We take a largely, not entirely, but a largely business approach to improving the educational experience of children while simultaneously improving your job satisfaction and making more money for you…sometimes a lot more money. You might think that all three of those things can't happen simultaneously, but I promise they can and they do. Here are a few examples to get you started.

a. There are directors in our industry that get paid $100,000 a year. They get paid that much because they're worth it. Even crazier, the owners of those centers are happy to pay them that much. Here's our first math lesson. You're the director of a center that makes a $200,000 a year profit for the owner after the owner pays you $40,000. You and the owner agree that you get 30% of all increases in profits (define profits clearly). You find a way to increase the profits by $100,000. You now have a $30,000 bonus and an income of $70,000 a year...it's a lot easier after you do it the first time. Oh, and the owner is making an additional $70,000 a year. What owner would ever say no to that deal? All you need to know is how to increase the profits. That's where we come in.

b. It's not magic. It's organization, execution and simple math. Here are a few tools to help you get there.

　　i. This book.

　　ii. Visit www.bfsvideos.tv for an entire video library on ways to make your center or school better, easier to run and more profitable.

　　iii. The BFS® website (www.bfsinc.net) has more FREE materials to help you succeed than any other early education consulting firm in the United States...maybe the world, but we didn't really check the whole world.

iv. Visit our Instant Q & A at www.bfsinc.net where you can choose any question and in three clicks watch video or read an article that will help you fix your issue. For example: How Do I Manage Problem Employees...three clicks and you're there. How Do I Limit Liability...three clicks and boom...you have eleven different ways to limit liability in your center or school.

Section 1
Managing

Avoiding The Pitfalls

How Do I Manage Problem Employees In My Childcare Center?

Problem employees are the ones that are constantly in your thoughts and robbing your mind of time and resources that are needed for the other factors that make your childcare company or school successful. One minute you want to fire them at the top of your lungs, and the next minute you're worried that they will call licensing or the Board of Education and lie about your school.

Over the last 20 years or so, I have discussed this exact problem with many clients and non-clients alike. Here's the good news...the irritation and anxiety can be remedied quickly, and it's not as difficult as you might think. Know that you are not alone. By far, the number one complaint nationwide for entrepreneurs in our industry is employees. Contrary to what you may have thought when you entered the business, it's not undisciplined children...it's not overprotective or overbearing parents...it's not even the occasional power happy licensing representative. It is employees.

STEP 1. Act, but act in a calm, organized, and focused manner. Don't let the problem linger as it will typically get worse if it goes unmanaged, and don't rush straight to "you're fired" as terminating the employee isn't always the answer either. There are many positive options between recognizing a problem and showing a potentially valuable employee to the door. So before you speak to the Problem Employee ("PE"), do the following:

1. Investigate the issue(s) or behavior(s) that is causing friction. Make sure you detach to the degree necessary to be objective. Base all of your thoughts and actions on facts—not gossip from teachers or other staff members and not preconceived results that aren't proven to have been caused by the PE. Things are not always as they appear. Two examples...I had discussions with two separate clients about two potential PEs. In the first client's center, the classroom video camera (no audio) made it appear that a teacher was very aggressively reprimanding a toddler. This circumstance was made worse because the child's mother was watching this action in real time in the center's office. The parent was furious...until she went into the room and heard her child's laughter because the teacher was playing with her son—not reprimanding him. In the second client's center, I was standing with the company president looking into a classroom through a two-way mirror. The employee was sitting as the children enjoyed some playtime around her. She wasn't terribly involved, but you don't have to be a gymnast to be a good teacher. Very quickly we determined that she wasn't involved with the children because she was falling asleep. Her head began to bob like a passenger on a long flight. She then laid her head face down on the table in front of her. The company president sent someone into the room to tell her to wake up...She did... and then she lit a cigarette. The first impression isn't always right so it's best to make sure you haven't decided the outcome of the meeting before the end of the meeting.

2. Decide whether you want to handle this matter alone or whether you need the assistance of HR personnel or an attorney. Many people handle these matters alone, but it's never wrong to be really well prepared.

3. Choose a time and place to talk with the PE. Pick a place where the PE will be most comfortable. The more comfortable the PE feels, the more likely it is that you will receive more and higher quality information. Remember, this circumstance may not be all about the PE. This is an opportunity for you to learn more about your company at the operational level. It's easy to write Standard Operating Procedures (SOPs). It's much harder to see if they work in the real world. Make sure you set aside more time than you think you'll need. You don't get that many opportunities to learn everything you can learn from a meeting like this one.

4. Put yourself in the right frame of mind before you step into the meeting with the PE. Make sure you are set to stay in your zone. The anxiety before this type of meeting is usually far more uncomfortable than the actual meeting, but you need to know that you can be engaged with the PE but detached just enough so you're not drawn into an emotional response or conversation. Your goals are two-fold - determine the facts and decide how to deal with the facts. You do not have to accomplish either or both of these goals in this first meeting.

STEP 2. Meet with the PE. In some cases, the misbehavior will be blatant, and the conversation will take on a more direct tone. However, in most cases the issue will be less obvious...maybe nonexistent. When you meet with the PE...

1. Put yourself on an even level with the PE. While this may not be true in the boss/employee relationship, it is true as people. At the end of the day, you are the boss and both of you know it. There's no need to accentuate this fact at this time.

2. Recognize the "person" without becoming emotional about it. Some employees respond to constructive criticism well while others are so critical of themselves that they respond much better to encouragement when they make a mistake.

3. When the moment comes, don't be afraid to step into the issue. The PE will know that something is coming. Waiting too long to discuss the point(s) will cause anxiety to rise and focus to decline for the PE and you. Be sincere. Be direct.

4. Whenever possible, ask open-ended questions. Remember, this is (first) a fact-finding mission for you. After you ask a question, stop talking. There may be an uncomfortable silence. Don't talk. Wait for as long as it takes. Most people have a tendency to want to talk and alleviate the awkwardness of the moment, but don't do it. The person across from you will talk.

5. After the PE begins to talk, let the PE talk until she/he has exhausted absolutely everything she/he can say. The more the PE talks, the more you learn. The more you learn, the better equipped you are to fix the issue with the PE. As a bonus, you may also learn things that will help you fix other parts of your company. These things can be as simple as stopping another "sleeper" PE from stealing supplies, to a director that is pocketing cash from unreported clients to systemic problems related to the Federal Food Program. It is very important to let the PE talk.

6. The issue is normally easier to fix after you have listened to the PE. If the issue is easy to fix, then fix it. Include the PE in your arrival at the solution. Make sure that it makes sense to the PE and that the PE is on-board with the solution. If the answer to the problem isn't clear, then don't fix it yet. Tell the PE that you appreciate the conversation; that you will take everything into consideration; and you will get back to her. Then get back to the PE as quickly as possible. It is nerve-racking for an employee to walk around with a cloud over her head. Her performance suffers, and she may convince herself that she needs to look for another job in spite of the fact that you want to keep her.

7. Consider the facts and decide on the best solution.

   a. Assuming the PE and the circumstance are salvageable, explain your expectations to the PE very clearly. Explain that you want the PE to be part of your mutual or collective work. Make sure the PE confirms they understand completely, and they are in complete agreement. If she is not in complete agreement or she seems unsure, flush out any hesitation to ensure that nothing has been missed. If something has been missed, ask questions and let the PE talk.

   b. If you decide that the PE needs to pursue their career path somewhere else, then I recommend that you consult with your HR department and/or an attorney educated and experienced in these matters. Some would say that it is overkill, but I have never talked with an officer or owner of a center or school that complained about being overly prepared. If you think that you have a PE that may be vindictive, you may want to have your attorney sit in on the meeting when the PE is dismissed as your attorney can explain to the PE that there will be consequences for any dishonest or vindictive acts.

STEP 3. Document everything during and/or after each meeting.

1. Create a written account of everything you've learned and how you can use it moving forward. This information is purely for you and appropriate management personnel.

2. Create an Employee Evaluation that includes (but is not limited to) a record of the PE's behavior before corrective action, the corrective action chosen and the PE's agreement to perform in accordance with the chosen and agreed upon corrective action.

3. It's best to have the evaluation signed by the PE so there is a written record for future reference in the event that additional correction or termination becomes necessary. The PE doesn't have to sign it, but a reluctance to sign the evaluation may indicate that the PE is not truly on board with the agreed upon corrective action or modifying her (or his) behavior.

These are guidelines to this process. There is no cookie cutter answer that fits every circumstance or every employee. Pay attention, listen to your instincts and execute. You'll be fine.

STAND FOR SOMETHING OR FALL FOR ANYTHING.

When I was in my 20s, I heard the saying…"Stand for something or fall for anything." I've always liked that saying. I think in some part, this saying has led me to my very black and white view of things. Since I was a kid, my mother has always tried to tell me that there are gray areas in life. To this day, we disagree on the point. There is right or wrong. Something is true or it's not true. I certainly understand that there are varying degrees of right and wrong, but at the end of the road it's still going to be right or wrong. We have always conducted business with this perspective. We do not flinch even when it might be more convenient to do so. Very rarely, but once in a while, we will learn that a client is lying to us. It's usually about the amount of money their company is making. Those clients are fired immediately. If a client makes a mistake, there is no problem. We'll find the mistake, fix it and move forward. But if the client purposely lies to us, there is no second chance. They're gone. Conversely, as long as our clients are doing business with character, we'll do most anything reasonable to take care of them. It's kind of an all or none policy. Whether it's a problem employee or a bigger issue, it's important to conduct business with character.

CHAPTER TWO

How Should I Structure My Childcare and Its Real Estate?

One, always talk with the proper professionals like your attorneys and CPAs before taking action. With that said, there are a number of smaller variables but only two basic ways to structure ownership of a childcare business component and its real estate. The childcare business and its associated real estate can be owned by the same entity or they can be owned by two separate entities. In most cases, it's better if the business component is owned by one company and the real estate is owned in a separate company. This structure allows for the following benefits:

1. As the real estate holding company (typically an LLC) will lease the real estate to the childcare business company, you have the ability to control or adjust the amount of the rent paid by the childcare company and received by the real estate company. This structure can be very helpful during tax planning.

2. Owning the business component and real estate in separate corporations can protect real estate holdings in the event someone sues the childcare business company. While we live

15

in a great country, we also live in an incredibly litigious country. You can't be too careful.

CHAPTER THREE

Being Prepared For An Emergency In Early Education

No one likes to think about bad things happening in any early education company, but everyone has the "nightmare" list. Oftentimes, it's this uncomfortable feeling that causes some people to avoid planning for these events. It simply becomes easier to focus on other parts of the business. The typical nightmare list includes the following:

- Child left on a bus or van

- Kidnapping

- Child gets off campus

- Child gets hurt in your school...or at home and you get blamed

- Violent parent in the building

- Bus or van is involved in traffic accident

- Anything bad that makes the local news

- Robbery

- Fire

- Tornado

- Hurricane

- Flooding

We have seen every one of these nightmares. Much like driving to work in the morning, we all know that someone will be in a serious accident every day, but we all believe it will happen to someone else. That's one of the beauties of the human psyche. Nonetheless, you still avoid being in the serious accident by…not following too closely, not texting, not reading the paper, not driving with your knees while you juggle breakfast…etc.

You are not in the accident because you are prepared if something "tries" to happen to you. It's no different for you and your early education company. While you can't avoid every accident, you can avoid nearly all of them when you're prepared.

Over the years, we have seen some genuinely good centers and schools damaged or ended by these very threats. All of these items can be managed effectively, and the answers are fairly obvious. The key is to be disciplined enough to make yourself insert the necessary and correct protective measures. If you don't already do it, you should perform your S.W.O.T. (Strengths, Weaknesses, Opportunities, and Threats) analysis at least once a year. If you have any questions about how to protect yourself and the people who depend on you, don't hesitate to see other BFS® publications (video, library, blogs, Instant Q&A…etc.) or consult with other appropriate professionals.

SOMETIMES WE SAVE THEM AND THEY'RE NOT EVEN CLIENTS

I think most people see the brokerage side of BFS® because that's the part that is most visible, but we do a lot of things to help people in the industry. Some things are profitable...some things are just about helping where it's needed. In some cases, we've spent time over several months to save schools and owners, and we didn't make a penny. Oftentimes, we've done the whole thing by phone and email. We never met them face-to-face, but we were there when they needed the critical information that saved them. We were there to teach them how to deal with overly aggressive banks or impatient landlords and other vendors.

Sometimes it's someone who is being sued by a parent and they're scared to death that word will get out and it will be the end of their school. In reality, it's usually a parent with some ambulance chasing attorney looking for an easy payday. It's amazing to see the ridiculous things people will invent to avoid working for their money. The fun part is getting to tell these owners that these things are usually kicked to the curb for nothing or settled for a nuisance value of somewhere between $500 and $2K. They seem instantly relieved. Sometimes they'll call back and tell me that everything worked out.

Of course, it's not completely altruistic...we're not a charity. I'd like to think that some of the schools we save or help will come back to us when they need our revenue generating services too.
One of the calls I like best is when someone calls years after we have helped them and says...You remember when I was in trouble...Well now I'm back...everything is good and we want to sell and retire...We want you guys to handle everything. They remember that we helped them when they really needed it.

CHAPTER FOUR

How To Limit The Liability In My Montessori School (Or Childcare Center)

There is always risk and opportunity for liability in a Montessori school, but there are a number of ways you can limit your liability and manage risk. (Always talk with the proper professionals before taking action.) Here are eleven things you may want to consider:

1. The Heart Stopper - Make sure you never lose track of a child. This terrifying event is most likely to happen when moving back and forth to the playground or when children are transported via busses or vans. Sometimes it is not enough to count the number of children. Make sure you perform a sweep after "all" of the children have left an area. This is especially important for busses and vans as children are easily overlooked when they are in the back of a bus or van.

2. Observe Good Business Practices - While it doesn't guarantee that you will be safe in your business environment, it certainly reduces the risk of getting sued.

3. **Business Component Incorporation** - Incorporate your business to limit your personal liability.

4. **Real Estate** - If you own real estate for your early education company, own it in a corporation or LLC that is different than the corporation that owns your business component. By holding your real estate in a different entity, it can be protected from litigation against the Montessori business company. Remember, you don't have to be wrong to be sued. Over the years, we have seen Montessori company owners sued frivolously for little more than a parent that just needed a source of income.

5. **Transportation** - While some companies don't go this far, owning your company vehicles in a separate transportation company helps to limit liability in the event of a traffic accident. The people of the U.S. make up approximately 4.5% of the world population. Meanwhile, the U.S. also has 90% of the world's lawyers. That's not an accident.

6. **Insurance** - Make sure you have the proper insurance coverage, including but not limited to, liability, property, flood and business interruption coverage.

7. **Teachers** - Train your teachers so they instinctively guard against any threat to the children, themselves or your school(s).

8. **Playgrounds** - Sectionalize playgrounds to make sure older children don't accidently collide with the little ones when playing outside.

9. Security - Install proper security doors and surveillance cameras so unwanted visitors don't gain access to your school or the people in it.

10. Licensing Compliance - While licensing is always part of the daily business of Montessori, keep in mind that the regulations are there with good purpose. Sometimes it is the smallest act of prevention that stops a catastrophe.

11. Professionals - Make sure you have at least one good attorney and one good CPA on your team. Having the right professional to show you the correct path is much easier and less costly than learning things the hard way.

By following a few practical and common sense rules, you can limit both your risk and your liability in your school.

CHAPTER FIVE

Avoiding Lawsuits In The Early Education Industry

Lawsuits in the United States are sometimes referred to as an epidemic. I've seen many lawsuits in our industry, and I've been asked to serve as an expert witness in many of those cases. While it's true that anybody can sue anybody, many lawsuits can be avoided. Here's the how and why of some of our industry's most popular litigation issues:

1. See Your Students - Whenever possible, look at the children as they enter your school. Say good morning to your parents. There was once an exceptional school built to provide early education for kids who otherwise had no chance at high quality early education. The people who founded the school had to chase the drug addicts out of the empty building so they could create the school. They created. They opened. They filled the school. The kids had uniforms so everyone was equal, and teachers were teaching. One morning, a parent drops off her son and exits the building quickly. Her son had been burned by what appeared to be an iron. She sued the school and claimed that one of the school's radiators burned her son. It hit the local news cycle. The school was gone

before they could get to a courtroom verdict. We were called in to sell the remnants. You can be right and still lose. Protect yourself.

2. Don't Provide Opportunities for the Opportunists - Sometimes parents fall on hard times. Most of us find a way to work it off, but sometimes people look for a shortcut. We've seen lawsuits filed against schools for…

   a. Woman in high-heeled shoes turns ankle walking back to car on level parking lot.

   b. Comments about an employee's clothing.

   c. Boy puts gravel in nose.

   d. Child falls on playground.

   e. Child bites child.

   f. Child hits child…and child hits child back.

   g. Slips on juice.

   h. Playground fence unsafe.

   These lawsuits are usually settled for the lower end of the $500 to $2,000 range, but they're still a drain on your time and energy.

3. Sexual Harassment - These cases aren't limited to men harassing women. If you're working in this industry, make sure you stay away from anything in this area. Unfortunately, even a

simple and genuine compliment can be used against you and your company if the wrong person is on the receiving end. In a meeting with an attorney, I was told of a case where four or five women sued the owner of the company for sexual harassment after working together for years. They were well into the lawsuit when the owner found and submitted several cards (birthday, etc.) containing sexual comments <u>from</u> these same women. The company won the lawsuit, but it cost tens of thousands of dollars and several long-term employees. Be polite. Be professional. Skip this whole experience.

Some lawsuits are legitimate and necessary. Many are not. For some attorneys, even if they know they can't win, they'll try to force some minor settlement if there is anything that looks like discrimination, harassment or neglect. For most people in our industry, these issues will never be a material problem. Be disciplined and professional on a daily basis. Everything should be fine.

Defending Your Profits

When Should I Raise Rates For My Montessori School (or Childcare Center)?

Every market is different and every Montessori school's circumstances need to be considered individually. However, it is very important to remember that the cost of living increases most every year. The cost of paying teachers increases most every year. If you are not increasing your rates at least once a year, you are simply paying these increased costs out of your own pocket.

Unless there are truly dire circumstances, rates should be increased by at least the cost of living or the teachers' raises every year - whichever is higher. While I understand that you may not want to raise rates, and that you may be placing the concerns of your clients (parents) ahead of your own needs, you should remember that the profits made by your school take care of your family.

From a purely financial viewpoint, the rule of thumb is…"If you raise your rates and no one leaves the school, then you didn't raise them enough."

CHAPTER SEVEN

How Do I Fix Collection Problems In My Childcare Center?

Collection problems can be sorted into two primary types. The first is collecting from private pay clients, and the second is collecting various subsidy funds from federal, state or local government.

Private Pay Clients (From 100% to Subsidy Differentials):
Private pay clients are sometimes like children who are simply testing boundaries. Operating in this mentality, the client will continue to take from you for as long as you will allow it. It is very important to set the boundaries (payment policy) when registering the parent's child or children. I can't count the number of times that a childcare company owner or officer has told me about a parent that can't pay tuition, but she drives a $50,000 car and she always has manicured nails. There will always be a reason that this parent can't pay their bill, and the more in arrears the parent becomes the less likely it is that you will ever recover the money owed to your company.

When the outstanding bill becomes too big to pay in the parent's eyes and you ask for the money owed to you, the parent simply stops coming to your school and moves on to the next school. Now you have to make the decision to pursue the parent through the legal system (typically small claims court), continuing calling their cell only to be ignored or forget the whole thing. None of these options are good as they are all time consuming and an expensive use of time that you could use for more productive activities like enrolling children with paying parents. Remember, while you are generously donating free childcare and education for the betterment of this parent's child, you still have to pay your bills–teachers, electricity, food…etc.

The most common collection policy used in professional childcare centers works as follows:

1. The tuition for the coming week is due no later than the Monday morning when the parent drops off their child.

2. If tuition is not paid by Friday of the same week, then the parent is not allowed to bring their child back until all tuitions are paid in full as defined in #1 above.

It's that simple. This structure is sometimes adjusted for a two-week period if you are in an area where parents have little disposable income and get paid every two weeks. However, I have never heard of a parent that can't make the weekly deadline when he or she decides to make the deadline.

If your collection policy is considerably more lenient than the one described above, then you may be wondering how to implement a new and stricter policy. As with any policy, it's always best in writing and preferably delivered so the parent can review it without the pressure of responding immediately. Hence, a letter in a sealed envelope works well. Ideally, the letter will also include other positive news about the center.

Remember, a policy is only as good as its execution so you'll want to be sure that your staff follows through and doesn't fall back into the old policy ways.

Government Subsidy Payments (GSP):
The owners, executives, shareholders and directors of our industry do not write policy for GSP. From the Federal Food Program to Title 20 to NACCRRA payments, we follow policy. Following policy carefully and quickly can improve your collection times. A few things that help our industry entrepreneurs are as follows:

1. Make friends with your contact person in the government entity that works with you. Whether it is face-to-face, by phone or email, make yourself stand out.

2. Part of making friends with your contact means making their job as easy as possible. That means that when paperwork is due, your paperwork is perfect and it's in the contact's hand the first minute you are allowed to submit it. You want to be seen as their easy school or center.

3. Ask questions and give your contact the opportunity to help you learn through his or her experience. The key to working well in any system is to understand the details of that system.

This industry is filled with good people. Unfortunately, some people try to take advantage of good people. You provide an incredibly valuable service for your parents and their children. A service that is likely more valuable than a parent realizes on any given day. A child's conditioning for a lifetime of education and success starts with the desire and ability to learn. There is no better investment for a caring parent than giving their child the ability to learn. It's important for your parents to understand this fact.

$4,000,000 AND HOLDING THE END OF THE ROPE

During the Great Recession years of 2008 to 2011, there were a lot of centers and schools in trouble. During these years we talked with (advised) many people for free. It was usually phone calls as most people are hesitant to send an email that says we're in trouble. Generally, it's bad business to work for free, but here we were doing the very thing we tell our clients not to do. During this time I really discovered just how connected we are to the industry. There were people calling us, sometimes in tears—men and women. I remember I talked with a guy one day. He called and he was holding it together, but I could tell that he was really stressed. He explained to me that he had begged, borrowed and put his entire savings ($4,000,000) into this one very nice center, and the center was dying right in front of him. He said no matter what he did, nothing was helping and the bank had been threatening to foreclose for a while. He was out of excuses. If he lost the school, he would lose everything, his business and his house, cars, the last of his savings…everything was on the block. He called me purely out of desperation. He was right. He had a problem. He actually had three problems. Problem #1: The bank was tired of listening to his excuses. Problem #2: His clients/parents were losing jobs so quickly that he couldn't replace the clients fast enough. Problem #3: He was trying to protect his teachers, but actually putting them in more danger.

We talked in detail, but I was pretty sure I knew the biggest problem from the start.

For Problem #1, I had him introduce me to his banker. We showed the banker BFS®'s track record and told him that if the bank would back off then BFS® would help him fix it. If for any reason we couldn't fix it, then the owner could have us sell it.

Either way, the bank stood to gain without the time and expense of going through a foreclosure. So, the bank was fixed at least for a while.

Problem #2 is if a parent wants to disenroll their child, you can't stop them. They have to do what they have to do. However, you can let them know that you're there for their child when they're ready to come back. You can also encourage them to come back earlier with incentives.

Problem #3 was the real problem. While the school's enrollment had continued to fall, he refused to layoff any teachers or cut their hours. I'm sure there were other minor issues, but this was the real problem. He didn't want his teachers to lose their jobs too. He was trying to protect them. I explained that I understood. Who doesn't want to protect teachers? They are the cornerstone for helping the kids. He was absolutely determined to keep his teachers. Finally, I explained that we could use different tools to save as many teachers as possible, but if he didn't do something, all of his teachers would lose their jobs because the bank will shut the doors if you can't show improvement. I showed him a combination of cutting hours, cutting hourly wages and increasing teacher duties so we could also cut the amount of work done by outside vendors.

It was great. He committed, followed our advice and it worked. The teachers kept their jobs. We helped save an entire school, and that is extremely cool.

CHAPTER EIGHT

Payroll and Your Montessori School or Childcare

Payroll expense is the single, largest expense for Montessori schools and childcare centers. It's also the expense that is most likely to get out of hand and ruin your profit margin.

Over the years, we've seen payroll costs (excluding payroll taxes) vary from a low of 38% of Gross Revenue to a high of more than 70% of Gross Revenue. Generally speaking, it should be about 45%. If it's higher than 50% of your Gross Revenue, then you should analyze the expense and make sure your funds are being allocated appropriately.

CHAPTER NINE

How To Reduce or Control Expenses In Your Early Education Company

Controlling and reducing the expenses of your childcare center or Montessori school starts with knowing what the expenses should be. Many company owners, presidents and CEOs started in this business with a vague knowledge of expense levels. They simply had enough tenacity to find something that worked before their company failed. Approximately 20% of new companies survive the first five years and discover a way to make it work. However, "making it work" is the absolute minimum of goals. There are very smart, hard-working people that have worked in the industry for 20 years or more and they are making it work. They have EBITDA margins that are 10% of gross revenue and they feel like they're doing okay. For 20 years they have been making 10%. Let's say that's $100,000 a year or $2,000,000 over 20 years. It is completely normal to produce a 20% EBITDA in our industry. For the same or less work over the same 20 years, each of these centers and schools could have been more effective and made $4,000,000. There is nearly always a way to improve your company's bottom line. Half of that equation is controlling expenses.

Here are some methods and ideas to help you with this side of your equation:

1. Shop your vendors aggressively every two years or when contract renewals permit. Don't settle for one or two bids from other vendors. If you can get ten bids from qualified vendors, then get all ten bids. At a minimum, it will give you a much clearer picture of the market cost for the service or product provided by each of the vendors. It is very easy to get comfortable with a vendor and choose to stay with the status quo, but this common occurrence can cost your company many thousands (maybe hundreds of thousands) of dollars over time...profits that should belong to your company, your family and you. One of the biggest and most popular expense reductions is eliminating moot vendors. For example, some centers and schools hire a janitorial service to clean classrooms in the evenings. In other more profitable centers and schools, teachers are responsible for making sure that their classrooms are clean and orderly at the end of the day. This practice often coincides with greater teacher pride and ownership of "their" classroom. The same can be said for the cook and kitchen...etc. Keep in mind that this is very light cleaning and organizing work. More difficult tasks such as buffing floors should be handled by professional cleaners... not teachers. Note that the cheapest price does not always mean that you should choose the vendor. Additionally, the vendor's first bid may not be the lowest bid. Don't be afraid to push vendors (from janitorial to banks) for better deals. I've never seen a vendor that has refused to work with a potential client because the client asked for a better deal. Remember, if you don't ask for it, the answer is definitely "No". Some vendors do cost more, and they're worth it.

However, shopping your vendors will give you far better information with which to make your decisions.

2. Make sure your payroll costs (not including payroll taxes) are no higher than 50% of your Gross Revenue. Payroll costs can be as low as 38% and as high as 50% of Gross Revenue and remain in the "normal" range. A very reasonable level is 45%. If payroll costs are over 50% for any reason, they should be reviewed and corrected. Corrected doesn't always mean cutting employees' compensation, but a review of the following items should be helpful.

   a. Payroll Creep. Payroll Creep occurs when employees have worked at the school for a number of years and received several pay increases during these years. While teachers and staff certainly should be paid fairly, annual pay increases are not guaranteed to anyone. A raise of fifty cents per hour for 20 full-time (40 hours) employees for five years costs your company and you $104,000 plus payroll taxes. To combat this issue you can choose to…give raises in alternating years…set policy that no one receives a raise until they have worked in the school for a minimum of one or two years…make raises performance-based or hire new, less expensive but competent teachers from the Early Childhood Education programs at local colleges and universities. From the other side of the equation, you can cover this cost by increasing your tuition rates, registration fees, supply fees, field trip fees, late fees, graduation fees, and/or transportation fees.

b. Ratio Watch. The Teacher Student Ratio should be checked every thirty minutes of the day. This practice may seem "impractical" until it becomes part of your daily routine. However, there are times of the day in every school when the school is not at its maximum attendance for the day. Most commonly, this occurs before and during morning drop-off, midday for centers or schools teaching morning and afternoon preschool classes and in the late afternoon when parents are picking up their children. During these times, there is no reason to have "extra" teachers on the payroll.

3. Target an Occupancy Cost (rent or mortgage) of 12% of Gross Revenues or less. There are three basic structures for occupancy cost: Your company pays rent to a third-party landlord; pays the mortgage to a bank/lender for the real estate; or pays rent back to you or your real estate holding company.

   a. Third-Party Landlord. Remember when you are negotiating a lease or the renewal of a lease with your third-party landlord, there are many negotiable terms in a lease and all of them can be used to negotiate lower rent. Some of these negotiable items are…the term of the lease…the term of lease extensions…the amount and frequency of rent increases…whether the rent increases are written in a way that is tax-friendly to the landlord, whether the lease is single, double or triple net…if triple net whether exceptions are made for expensive items like the roof or HVAC. There are plenty of options for reducing rent.

b. Bank Mortgage. Similar to the third-party lease above, a mortgage has many negotiable terms to be utilized. However, negotiating with a bank can be much easier. In 3.a. above and unless you're willing to move your company's operations, you are limited by the fact that you can only negotiate with the one landlord. But, you can move your mortgage to any bank that is willing to meet your terms. With the exception of gathering your own information, the banks do all the work and you get to make the decision. Banking is an exceptionally competitive business, and nothing is better for the consumer than competition amongst vendors. Banks are eager to secure good loans and improve their own portfolios. Amongst the negotiable factors to be used in a loan conversation are...the amount of the interest rate, whether the rate is fixed or variable, points, how much collateral, what type of collateral, how long the collateral can be held (Banks would have you believe that collateral must be held for the entire term of the loan, which is not true in most cases.), if prepayment penalties apply, the amount of prepayment penalties, the time period for which prepayment penalties would apply and whether the loan is assumable...to name a few.

c. Leasing Property Back to Yourself. When you or an entity that you control serves as the landlord, you have more flexibility. You can choose to increase or decrease the rent to your center or school. Adjusting the rent paid by your center or school to your real estate entity (LLC, corporation or personal ownership) allows you the flexibility to reduce your tax burden (income and payroll taxes) while increasing income to you.

4. Organize and shop to keep food and supplies cost below 6% of Gross Revenue. Food costs can normally be kept below 4% while feeding the children well. The supplies (plates, napkins, plastic ware, cups…etc.) associated with food can be purchased for 2% of Gross Revenue. Beyond the obvious task of shopping at the wholesale clubs, try the following:

   a. Look for area organizations that connect entrepreneurs for greater purchasing power.

   b. Review organizations that you may already belong to as some of these organizations may have this type of benefit for you but it isn't listed as the primary benefit of the organization.

   c. Shop online for nonperishable items

   d. Form your own group to assist in buying in bulk. The group only needs to have the common interest. It does not have to be made solely of early education companies.

   e. Negotiate prices with vendors based on your minimum annual purchasing with the vendor. For example, if you know that you spend $1,000 per month on art supplies, that's fine. However, you may be able to get better pricing if you negotiate with your vendor based on a guarantee that you will buy a minimum of $12,000 of supplies annually.

5. Keep the cost of utilities under 3% of Gross Revenue. While there is less flexibility in shopping utilities, there are ways to control these costs.

    a. Where the option exists, shop utility providers against one another. The cost of trash and snow removal can change materially in short periods of time as a larger number of smaller vendors compete for market share.

    b. Take advantage of discounts for early payment.

    c. When appropriate and safe, open the windows and turn off the heat or air conditioning.

6. Balance your advertising cost with effectiveness. The goal here is simple. Create the maximum desired enrollment without spending any money. This goal, of course, sounds ridiculous. However, it is possible or very, very nearly possible. There are centers and schools that operate at or very close to full enrollment and spend almost nothing (less than $1,000 a year) on advertising. Generally speaking, on day one you start with no enrollment and you have to pay for a lot of advertising. As you progress, these two items flip based on the quality of the centers or schools you build. The real key is to track your advertising results so you know where you should and should not spend your money.

    a. Advertising options include but are not limited to the following:

        i. Word of mouth from current and previous clients...Best Ever.

ii. Every single teacher and other staff member who works in your company. If your people know that "their" center is a great center, they can tell others the same…and people recognize truth when they hear it.

iii. One of the best things to happen to advertising is digital advertising, also referred to as Internet marketing. Everything from your website to your newsletter to your daily or weekly parent updates can be produced and distributed for minimal cost. There is never a situation where all of your advertising should be online, but this option helps you to lower costs while you push for full enrollment and zero advertising costs.

iv. Local paper publications and their online work.

v. Newsletters of larger local employers.

vi. Publications distributed in your local elementary schools.

vii. There are many other types of advertising, but these effective options are amongst the least expensive.

SAVING CLIENTS FROM BANKRUPTCY

When I think about many of the people and companies that we have worked with over the years, it seems much the way a teacher remembers her students. Teachers will tell you that the students who stand out are the ones who were either very good, very bad, or made remarkable improvement. The same is true for me when I think of the owners, executives and directors that we have served.

One of my favorites is a client in Massachusetts some years ago. When we talked the first time, he was very direct and very honest about his situation. This is my favorite type of person—direct, honest and no pretentious ego. He said that the bank was about to foreclose and take his center...he was about to have to turn away nearly 100 children and their parents, and you could tell it was very personal to him. It wasn't a simple black and white, profit or no profit decision. By his own words, he said after nearly 16 years he was facing foreclosure and his options were extremely limited. He understood the pieces, the business and real estate, but he couldn't turn it around and couldn't sell it before the bank took everything. This is one of my favorite games to win. Our client feels like they are a complete underdog to the bank...like the bank controls what's going to happen to them, and then we flip the dynamic and the client wins anyway. Actually, everybody wins - including the bank. Contrary to what a bank oftentimes wants you to think in these scenarios, they usually do not want to foreclose. They just want their money. The key is to show the bank that there is a better way for them to get their money. I mean really, who doesn't want an easier way to get money.

In the early years, it was tricky to save a client from a bank. This was before people could see the BFS® track record. It was before people knew that we always do exactly what we say we're going to do. Bankers have heard every story in the world from people who have found their way into a difficult position. It all starts to sound like the dog ate my homework. Our approach when saving our clients from banks is to make sure the bank understands, we're not just saving our client, we're saving the bank too—at least on this deal. The immediate, macro decision to be made by the bank is to foreclose or not to foreclose. If they foreclose, they incur the costs related to the foreclosure until such time as they can flip the property. Pending the circumstances, they may or may not get enough from the sale to recoup the defaulted loan, legal costs and crazy amounts of fees and penalties they stack on top of our clients. Our proposal to the bank is...Why would you take these risks and incur these costs when we (BFS®) can manage the whole thing, get a materially higher price, improve the odds that you'll get all of your money, and it won't cost the bank a penny. What banker in his or her right mind would ever say no to a deal like that!?! All the banker has to do is give our client a little time and stay out of the way. Generally speaking, I like bankers. They're smart, quantitative thinkers. Problems are black and white—no gray. That's perfect for us. I'm not crazy about some banking/financial institution practices at the higher levels. On a national and global level, these otherwise conservative looking institutions make some really big bets, and we the taxpayers end up covering the shortage when they can't clean up their own mess. It is the only industry I can think of where making a bigger mess gets you better terms on fixing the issue. Think banking collapse of 2008, think Savings and Loans crises, think 1980s U.S. banks lending to Latin American countries (Argentina, Brazil, Mexico and Venezuela)...think Great Depression. Regardless, our client only had a problem with one bank and we were fortunate to be working with a smart banker. He understood...he gave us space...we went to work...turned the company around...increased its value and sold it for top dollar in an all-cash deal. The bank got its money, but more importantly our client moved from a position of turning nearly 100 families into the street and being marked with a foreclosure to improving the center for the parents, children and staff, paying off all of his debt, putting money in his own pocket and ensuring that the center would continue to serve the community after his departure. Very, very rarely do I have a bad day, but when I do, I think about clients like this one.

CHAPTER TEN

Designing Your Childcare or School Space

Utilizing every inch of your school in the most effective way possible will provide a much better environment for the children, the parents, the teachers, and your profitability.

Efficiency is one of the traits that promotes and inspires professionalism. Professional ownership promotes professional management which promotes better teachers which promotes more attentive, happier and better-educated children. A well-designed, professionally functional school will stand out next to most competitors. Separating your school from your competition earns you…more clients. It's key to know that most anyone can do something 90% right. It's pushing for the last 10% that separates you from the pack. Designing your space correctly is one of the items commonly overlooked in the first 90%.

When you're designing or redesigning your space, keep the following items in mind:

1. Try to make at least 80% of your internal space licensed, classroom space. It's very easy to think that wide hallways

look good. They do, but too wide may mean losing licensed space and profits.

    a. For example, if you have a school hallway structure and you make your 60-foot hallway four feet wider than required (very common) then you give up 240 square feet (SF) that could have been used for classroom space.

    b. 240 SF divided by 35 SF per child equals the loss of room for 6.86 more children.

    c. Assuming weekly tuition of $125 for 52 weeks a year, you give up $44,571 in annual revenue.

    d. Over ten years, that's $445,710 in revenue.

    e. If you have an EBITDA (cash flow) of 20% of revenue, then you have given away $89,142 that could have been income to you and your family.

    f. That's for just two feet on each side of one hallway.

2. Avoid the big office giveaway. Unless you have a large management staff actually using the big office, then the best office is the one that contains your necessities (desk, computer, printer, space to talk with parents). Otherwise, your office can become very expensive real estate.

3. When possible, place your school on the "morning" side of the street. This means that you want to be on the side that parents are most likely to travel on their way to work. Anything that saves a working parent time or effort is helpful.

4. Place your school close enough to the road to be seen but not so close that passing cars become a perceived danger.

5. Think daily operations as you design or have your school designed. Nobody wants a bathroom next to the kitchen.

6. If you can, provide drive-up coverage so rainy days don't cause mom or dad to take a second shower.

7. Keep in mind that you don't have to build a $3,000,000 school to make these things work. They can be done on a budget or modified to improve your school even if your school is smaller or less elaborate.

These are just a few of the ways to improve the design of your school and increase your profitability. Listen closely to your teachers, other staff and parents. Some of the best ideas come directly from the front lines.

CHAPTER ELEVEN

What Should I Expect When A New Childcare Center or School Opens Close To Me?

Here are ten things you should expect when a new competitor opens close to your school:

1. Private chatter amongst your parents.

2. Private chatter amongst your staff.

3. Both parents and staff asking you what you think of the new place.

4. Your new competitor will check your tuition rates and business practices.

5. Your new competitor may try to hire your staff members—anyone from your cook to your director.

6. Some of your parents or staff may leave and go to the new center.

7. Some of your parents or staff will come back from the new center.

8. Some new competitors will undercut your tuition rates initially, and then raise their rates after they get established.

9. If the new competitor is doing anything better than you, then you'll have the opportunity to check your new competitor and improve your own game.

10. If your new competitor brings new traffic to the area, then you'll have the opportunity to secure additional clients for yourself.

The ten items above are very normal, and each can be managed effectively. Many of your strategies will be based specifically on your market and the similarities and differences between you and your new competitor. Oftentimes, competition will push us to be better than we thought we could be.

CHAPTER TWELVE

The State Is Cutting Our Subsidy. What Should I Do?

Unfortunately and in spite of all of the political promises for education money, state governments also operate within the U.S. economy. When our economy declines, state governments adjust their budgets too. If your enrollment is 100% private pay, then you're not worried, but only a small percentage of centers and schools are 100% private pay.

The situation can be difficult, but this problem has to be managed like any other. You need to make sure your company is positioned properly or you need to reposition it if you're already caught in the net of a funding cut. Sometimes early education companies wait to see when their state government is going to return to higher reimbursement rates. Don't wait. The state government will do whatever it does whenever it chooses to do it. You can make decisions to improve your operations and profitability now. Everything the state does will be additional profits on top of the improvements that you will have already made. During down times, I have seen states cut rates when the state budget got too tight. I have also seen states where there have been huge increases in state subsidy. These increases have caused some BFS® clients to reap large windfall profits. Remember, the pendulum swings both ways, but you can't usually time the pendulum. Here are some options to help you:

1. Talk with other owners who have the same problem and take your collective concerns to your state and local politicians. While this may sound like a generic, go-nowhere answer, it does work. No politician wants to be on the news for taking education and care away from young children. Over the years, we've had many clients that were facing cuts in subsidy rates. Sometimes the rate cuts were implemented by government. Almost without exception, given enough time and consistently applied pressure, the rates have been returned to earlier higher levels.

2. Assuming your state allows it, increase the portion of the fee paid by subsidized parents to compensate for some or all of the loss in tuition reimbursements from the state.

3. Increase other fees…

   a. Field trips fees.

   b. Supply fees.

   c. Registration fees.

   d. Graduation fees.

   e. Transportation fees.

   f. Tuition to private pay clientele.

4. Increase marketing to private pay clientele to help balance your clientele and become less dependent on subsidy reimbursement.

5. Search for other local, state or federal programs that can be helpful to your company. Remember, there are programs beyond subsidized tuition and the Federal Food program. You just have to do the research.

CHAPTER THIRTEEN

How Much Should My Major Expenses Be For My School or Childcare Center?

You may find it surprising to learn that <u>many</u> people in the early education industry have never truly known how much some of their primary expenses should be. Oftentimes, people come into the business and find a way to make it work and then we stop looking for ways to continue improving. You can use the table below to see if you can improve the performance of your own school. The "Industry Normal" amounts below are based on information gathered directly from centers and schools across the U.S. To calculate your own percentages, simply divide your expense amount by your Gross Revenue. These ranges are typical norms, but better results are possible in many cases.

	Actual	Industry Norm
Salaries/Wages for Employees	_____%	**45% – 50% Maximum**
Occupancy Cost (Rent or Mortgage)	_____%	**12%**
Food and Food Related Supplies (Plates, Napkins…)	_____%	**6%**
Utilities	_____%	**2% – 3%**

It may help you to know that this simple table has helped countless people improve the profitability of their centers and schools. Remember, a small percentage change over time can mean a material improvement in dollars to you. If you choose, additional profits also provide you with the option of reallocating funds to better programs for the kids.

CHAPTER FOURTEEN

How To Handle A Minimum Wage Increase In The Early Education Industry

As payroll costs are the single largest expense in a center or school, many company owners and executives are concerned with the potential increase in the minimum wage. No one likes to see increases in expenses without corresponding increases in revenues and profits. Here's a few ways to deal with an increase to the minimum wage:

1. Don't panic. This wouldn't be the first time our industry has seen an increase in the minimum wage. It's not fatal. It's just an adjustment.

2. Do the math and determine how much your payroll will increase with the wage increase. Don't forget to include the corresponding increase in payroll taxes. If you know the amount of the increase in your expenses, you'll be better at making up the difference…maybe more.

3. Raise your rates. The minimum wage increase won't be a secret to your parents. You can raise your tuition rates (and other fees like Registration, Supplies, Fieldtrip…etc.) to cover

some or all of the wage increase. It is more difficult to raise rates in some centers than others. In some cases it will be better if you use smaller, but multiple rate increases to help your parents get through the change.

4. This is another good catalyst for shopping your vendors.

5. Ask your employees to give you suggestions about reducing costs. Your employees are often closer to the source of the waste so they recognize it sooner. Get everyone involved in the team effort. If enough additional profit is created, pay a bonus to the employee(s) who find smart ways to save money. Award the bonus in front of the team. It should be clear that good ideas are encouraged and rewarded.

6. Invest in technology. New technologies from inventory control to student-teacher ratio tracking to social media allow for lower costs, better service and more clients.

If you're diligent about these practices, you may find that an increase in the minimum wage leads you to higher profits.

CHAPTER FIFTEEN

How To Hire Great Long-Term Staff For Your Early Education Company

Every industry has its challenges. In the early education ("EE") industry, the challenge is to find and keep good teachers and directors. However, there are many EE companies that get and keep great teachers and directors for many years. These schools have very little staff turnover, and they are profitable. The primary key is to avoid looking for teachers and directors. Look for the teacher or the director. Then, repeat the process for every teacher and director thereafter. I hear you saying, "Yes, Brad, that couldn't be more obvious." In this industry, most EE companies pursue en masse and very few good directors or teachers get the special treatment. The best teachers and directors are worth the extra effort. Treat them like you're hiring executives and keep them long term. EE companies run ads and hope for responses. When is the last time you were trying to hire someone and took them to an expensive restaurant for dinner? When was the last time you met with a candidate, and you knew something material about them that wasn't on their resume? People want to feel that their work matters…that they matter. Contrary to traditional thinking, money is not the only thing that matters.

Here are a few steps you can take to find your ideal teacher or director:

1. Write the most detailed description of the most perfect director or teacher you could ever hope to hire. Leave the description alone for at least 24 hours. Go back and make the description better. Repeat this process until you can't possibly make the description any better.

2. Write the plan for finding this candidate. Include the places you'll search and the contacts and tools you'll use. Again, leave it alone for at least 24 hours. Go back repeatedly and make the plan better until you can't make it better. This procedure will become a SOP (Standard Operating Procedure) for you. Within your plan for finding candidates, be sure to include the following items:

   a. Always ask every non-interested candidate for referrals to other potential candidates.

   b. Offer a finder's fee for the person you hire.

   c. Always keep information on the people who are not interested. "Not interested" today doesn't mean not interested tomorrow. If you have a nonaggressive means of staying in contact with these people (for example, your monthly newsletter), use it.

   d. Don't be afraid to ask any candidate what would make their current position better. Maybe you have or can create "better".

3. Apply for grants so your company can afford to pay more and get the better teachers and directors. (See our Resources Page at www.bfsinc.net for access to grants.) Grants are one of the fastest ways to transform a school. I've seen clients secure grants as high as $740,000 for a single center. This is a real option.

4. Use social media to network in the education sector.

5. Find out who your staff knows. If you have a "star" on your staff, chances are high they know other "stars". Referrals from within the walls of your EE company are excellent places to find ideal candidates. Note, the quality of the referral is usually similar to the quality of the employee referring.

6. Script your interview process. When you get that great candidate in front of you, be prepared to run a professional interview. Remember, if they're good, they're interviewing you too.

While you always have to be in ratio, one really good employee is worth three average employees. Good ideas, program improvement, greater profits and necessary vacations come from hiring exceptional people—not the average. We know that in the real world, good people are hard to find, but they are worth the effort if you want an exceptional company…and a better night's sleep.

Once you have used your system to find one really good director or teacher, repeating your process will become easier.

GENUINELY THOUGHTFUL CLIENTS

Some of the people we work with are especially thoughtful. I have received many invitations to weddings of our clients' children, birthdays, general parties or dinner whenever I can get to their city - occasionally whenever I can get to their country. The early education community is a good place to be.

CHAPTER SIXTEEN

How To Increase The After Tax Income Of Your Early Education Company

Notes:

1. Most U.S. taxpayers overpay their taxes.

2. At the time of this writing, the IRS tax code has 74,608 pages, and it is constantly changing.

3. You should always pay your tax bill.

4. You should never pay a tax bill that isn't yours to pay.

Don't just send your numbers to your accountant or CPA firm and wait to get your tax news. I'm involved in conversations with the owners and executives of early education companies most every day. Most every day I hear that these smart, successful people are not telling their CPAs about expenses that can be written off on their company tax returns. As the tax code will likely change between this writing and the time you read this page, we won't discuss specifics here. Instead, every time you discuss taxes with your financial professional, try to have at least one item where you ask your CPA if something is tax deductible. There is no downside to asking. If you ask ten times and you're right once, you just might increase your income materially for years to come.

Remember, a dollar saved (from taxes) is better than a dollar earned. You work really hard for your money. There is no reason to give it away after you've done the toughest part of the work.

CHAPTER SEVENTEEN

Know How To Count Your Money In Early Education

Whenever professionals discuss the financial performance of early education companies, the conversation will always include "cash flow"…and that can be dangerous. The term "cash flow" means different things to different people, and it can be the cause of material misunderstandings that lead to losing money, litigation or both.

Instead of using the term cash flow in your discussions, use the term EBITDA. EBITDA means…

Earnings

Before

Interest

Taxes

Depreciation and

Amortization (of non-tangible assets—not loan amortization)

It is commonplace for Earnings to include compensation paid to the company's owners including salary and benefits like the owner's health insurance, company car…etc.

EBITDA is a much better indicator of a company's true cash flow and its ability to meet its obligations as it includes the noncash tax deductions of Depreciation and Amortization. EBITDA shows you how much money you have, not how much you have on paper.

ALWAYS: If you're in a conversation with someone who uses the term "cash flow", ask them if they are defining cash flow as EBITDA…or simply ask them how they are defining cash flow. Many sales people like to use the term cash flow. It's vague. It allows for a lot of latitude. People depend on you. It's always best to be very clear when you're talking about your money.

CLIENT GETS $5OOK EXTRA AND ASKS FOR FEE CUT—A reminder that it's still business.

Some years ago we were retained by a client. As always, I met with the client and evaluated the schools. The client and her financial advisor were thrilled with the amount of the evaluation. They even commented that they felt like the asking price might be too high, but they would be very happy to get a price in that range.

At the end of the day we produced a solid buyer and because of the way we structured the transaction, our client received about $500,000 more than the full asking price. If someone does this kind of job for me, I'm thinking that I might pay that person a bonus. I firmly believe that people who do exceptional work deserve exceptional rewards. In this particular case, instead of offering a bonus (not expected) or just saying thank you, our selling client waited until just before closing and threatened to back out of the deal if we didn't cut our fee. Setting aside the legal ramifications for a minute, I informed our suddenly greedy teammate that it was within her power to terminate the deal, but she and her advisor would be keeping their word and paying our fee as agreed. The closing was completed. Our client received more than she had hoped. We did not cut our fee. I can think of no industry that I would rather be in, but no matter your part in the industry, it is still a business—not a charity.

CHAPTER EIGHTEEN

More Money and Less Debt For Your Early Education Company

If you own the real estate for your early education company, all of the following improvements can be made with just one change:

1. Increase your profits.

2. Increase the market value of your business.

3. Lower your occupancy cost.

4. Eliminate or reduce your debt.

5. Increase your cash holdings.

6. Decrease your taxes.

7. Increase the number of buyers qualified to buy your company.

8. Continue to use the same facility(ies).

9. Expand your early education company faster.

10. Move toward retirement without doing it all in one step.

The one change is…Sell your real estate and keep your business. It's called a Sale and Leaseback, and it's done all the time. You can sell your real estate and simultaneously secure a lease under your terms and accomplish everything on the list above. Here's a typical example to show the difference with and without real estate.

Let's say you're going to invest $2,000,000 in a childcare center or school. You spend $600,000 (3 X EBITDA) for a business component that produces a return (EBITDA) of $200,000 a year and $1,400,000 for the real estate. Your annual return on investment for the business component is 33% ($200,000/$600,000). At the time of this writing, the average return on unleveraged commercial real estate is 8.8% per the National Council of Real Estate Investment Fiduciaries (NCREIF). So on a pre-tax basis, $2,000,000 invested at 33% yields $660,000 a year to you. Two million dollars invested at 8.8% yields $176,000 a year to you. It's true that you might also be building equity in the real estate, but it is highly unlikely that the real estate equity will make up the difference between 8.8% and 33% annually.

This isn't a new idea. According to JLL's U.S. Investment Outlook, 2018 saw strong commercial real estate activity as transaction volumes reached $481 billion. Overall interest in net-lease assets remained robust. The sector recorded $44.1 billion in transactions, of which sale-leaseback transactions represented nearly 15% (about $6.6 billion). Companies continue to hedge against market uncertainties through sale-leaseback transactions, in which an owner/occupier sells real estate and then leases it back from the purchaser.

Many of the largest and most successful early education companies in the country utilize this practice to better their companies…So can you.

Best People Best Centers

CHAPTER NINETEEN

Leadership In Your Childcare Center or School

Whether you are an owner, director or both in a childcare center or a school, your leadership skills will determine your success in this industry. There are several key traits that every successful owner has developed over their career. Here is a short list of items to consider if you want to become a great leader within your early education environment.

Vision - Having a clear vision for creating and perfecting your center or school is important if you want to enjoy the fruits of your labor. Vision requires more than passion. It requires relentless focus and rewards you accordingly.

Delegation - In some centers and schools, this is a difficult task for owners and directors. They want to do everything themselves to make sure it's "done right". Give up a little control and let your staff do their jobs. The key is to remember that you work ON your company not just IN it. Hire the right people for the right job, then manage. You don't have to kill yourself with 14-hour days to be successful in the industry.

Culture - The culture of a school begins with its ownership and management. Nearly all of your staff will follow the culture they experience when they are hired. Your ability to hire well and require the respectful conduct of a professional workplace will permeate each new hire...as will the disrespectful conduct of a bad hire. Ownership means acceptance of risk. Hiring well is the best way to manage employee risk.

Trust your instincts - Most of the time, an owner knows the right answer when she takes the time to listen to that inner voice. If an owner has been in business for five years or more, then the "inner voice" becomes the "voice of experience". If the owner has been in business less than five years, then it is especially important to listen to the inner voice including the voice that says "Find professional help." Pay attention, listen to yourself carefully and then trust yourself.

Self-Evaluation - Think about your current leadership qualities. Do an honest assessment of your strengths and weaknesses. Once you can compensate for your own strengths and weaknesses, you will find your day-to-day work to be less stressful and your school will become the vision you've chosen.

You may not know the answer to every question at every minute of every day, but these practices will keep you moving in the right direction.

Princess

One of the most wasteful and unfortunate circumstances is when we get the call to save a princess. I have seen parents spend two, three, four million dollars to buy a center or school for their daughter. The truth is the daughter doesn't want to work that hard. After two or three years of taking losses, someone (usually dad) calls us to fix the school. It can go either way. Sometimes the princess will find her character, pull up her bootstraps and go to work. Sometimes, we will give very specific, easily executable directions to fix the school and nothing happens. The school struggles a little longer...Mom and Dad close it and sell the real estate. It really is a waste. It could have been another really good school improving the chances for more kids. If you're going to operate in this industry, work ethic is a requirement.

CHAPTER TWENTY

Selecting The Right Team For Your Early Education Company

It's been said that when opening and operating any business, you must have the right people, doing the right things, at the right time. It seems simple, but 80% of new businesses still fail in the first 60 months—not five years, 60 months. New companies don't fail in five years. They succeed or fail one month, one day, one hour and one decision at a time. You can succeed or fail faster or slower, but at the base, it still happens one decision at a time. The key to making good decisions is having the best information. It all starts with the "right people".

1. Decision One: You. It's important to know and be honest about your own strengths and weaknesses. By being candid with yourself, you identify the gaps and you more readily recognize not just the people you need but the personalities you need. For example, you may be brilliant but not particularly assertive. Hence, you look for more assertive directors, assistant directors and attorneys.

2. Decision Two: Attorney. Most of us know a few attorneys, but your friend who practices family law is not the person to

help you navigate zoning laws, negotiate leases or handle your mergers and acquisitions work. Pick an attorney who has a significant, documented history of success in the right field. If you don't know an attorney with the type of experience you need, start with the most successful, non-competitor, business people you know and ask them who they use. If you don't feel that the referral to the attorney is strong enough, don't hesitate to ask attorneys for references. Some attorneys will tell you that they can't give you references because of attorney client privilege. Of course there is attorney client privilege, but most any experienced attorney can produce references when they need to do so.

3. Decision Three: CPA. If you're going to make money, you need to be able to account for it and protect it from inappropriate taxes. A good CPA will save your money from taxes, and those savings compounded over years in business can determine the decade in which you retire.

4. Decision Four: Director. If you're not going to be the director/administrator of the school, then this position will be the most important operational staffing decision you'll make. An average director can maintain a good school. A great director with autonomy can make an average or bad school great. A bad director can ruin anything. I always found that high-quality directors are worth a premium when it's necessary. This is not the place to pinch pennies.

5. Decision Five: Banker. If you're going to borrow money, and most people do, you need to have one reliable banker for knowledge and insight and another 15 or so to make sure the first banker is giving you the best terms possible when you borrow. Failing to provide a competitive environment for

your banker(s) can be extremely expensive to you. A difference of a quarter percentage point on a million dollar loan over 20 years costs you and extra $34,793. The U.S. has a lot of banks. It's a competitive business. There's no reason not to use them correctly.

6. Decision Six: Real Estate Transaction Professionals. If you're buying property (land and/or buildings) and you're not experienced in transactional work, get professional help to ensure that you won't miss important factors in the transaction. Help can come in the form of your CPA, a real estate attorney and/or an experienced broker.

7. Decision Seven: Marketing Professional. This decision can be more difficult as many people have trouble defining marketing. In today's environment, you must have an Internet presence. Make sure your marketing person is a talented SEO (search engine optimization) person. You can also learn about many tested, successful marketing options by visiting the many free resources at www.bfsinc.net.

8. Decision Eight: IT professional. You will need computers so you will need an IT professional. It is better if this person is not part of your staff as some of the information exposed during the work may be sensitive and not to be shared with the director or teacher who is "good with computers." While vendors (attorneys, CPAs, bankers, IT professionals) have an inherent duty to maintain your privacy, you should never be reluctant to have your vendor(s) sign a non-disclosure agreement.

9. Decision Nine: Payroll. There are several good payroll companies. None of the major companies should have any

problem managing your payroll. They're not terribly expensive, and if you have ever talked with anyone who botched their payroll taxes, then you know they are worth the cost.

10. Decision Ten: Hire your directors, administrators, teachers, drivers and cooks and go to work.

The early education industry is a great industry, but it requires real work and it doesn't allow much room for error. Don't put yourself at a disadvantage. Your competition won't. Remember…the Right People Doing the Right Things at the Right Time.

BAD PARTNERS

Sometimes we get calls from a partner (sometimes more than one partner) who owns centers or schools, and they are fighting with their business partners. Sometimes the calls are pre-litigation and sometimes they're already deep into an expensive legal fight. These fights are much like some failing marriages in that the participants have oftentimes become very emotional. They're not making logical decisions. Their focus has become wholly centered on taking from the other person or trying to hurt the other person in some way.

While we're never going to hang a shingle to be the Corporate Marriage Counselor for Early Education, it's important to be rational and logical during these unfortunate circumstances. I've seen these fights become so vicious that they have driven the companies or at least some of their centers into closing their doors. Nobody goes into a partnership thinking it will fail, but when it's time to terminate the partnership, there is no reason to hurt the schools.

CHAPTER TWENTY-ONE

Building A Team For Your Childcare Company or School

When you consider the teachers and other staff members in your school, it's important that you think of them as a cohesive unit. I recognize that we have a lot of turnover in the industry, so it is basically impossible to have a cohesive team that includes everyone in your company. However, it is very possible to have a core group of employees consisting of your administrator, director, assistant director and your best teachers. When you have a core team that you trust, it makes the school run better, and it gives you more time to focus on other things—like growing your company...or going to the beach.

So, here we go:

1. Create an environment that encourages sharing and working together to improve your school. Try to avoid hiring the "show up, do your work and get your paycheck" candidates. You may not spot them in the interview process, but it isn't too tough to see it during their probationary period. By far, the number one complaint I hear from the owners of early education centers and schools is...They cannot stand the in-house bickering amongst staff members. A mentally

healthy environment created by the right people, doing the right things at the right time will lead to better staff retention and higher profits.

2. Acknowledge teachers when they do something good. Most everyone likes positive recognition. Whether we're two or fifty-two, recognition is appreciated.

3. Keep the communication channels open. It's important for the teachers and other staff to trust you and each other.

4. Have clear expectations for everyone involved in your center or school. Make sure each of your staff members confirm their understanding of your expectations.

5. Learn how to delegate responsibilities. Delegation provides a sense of pride for the trusted employee and a shorter to do list for you.

6. Hold your staff members accountable. It's not enough to delegate or explain expectations; the job has to get done.

These simple steps can help you improve morale in your centers or schools and, by extension, build the kind of relationships you want to have with your teachers, children and parents.

CHAPTER TWENTY-TWO

Montessori Teaching Growing Faster In U.S.

Here's why. "Montessorians", like many good teachers of all types, believe in their work. They believe in their founder and her principles. Dr. Maria Montessori, the first woman medical doctor in Italy (1896), was also learned in biology, psychiatry and anthropology. The attention of her accomplishment led to an appointment by Italy's Minister of Education, and this appointment gave Dr. Montessori the chance to work with children. She worked with children from the poorest areas of Italy, some of which were cognitively challenged. With her scientific discipline and relentless tenacity, these poor kids, including those with greater challenges, were able to pass standard testing with above-average scores. Her studies of educational methods included boys and girls from races and cultures all over the world. It was through these studies that she found and declared two principles that are the foundation of Montessori teaching. To simplify, they mean...One, children as a group have universal characteristics. Two, each child is truly unique and should be accepted, respected and admired as one of life's genuine treasures.

Today, Montessori can be found working throughout the world. In the United States, Montessori went to work in the mid 1960s. It grew slowly but since 2000, the use of Montessori teaching methods has more than doubled in formal channels. Additionally, there are many other schools where Montessori programs have been implemented, and still more centers and schools that borrow from the Montessori philosophy.

Whether she realized it or not, Dr. Montessori wasn't just an agent for change in global education. She was the architect for the infrastructure that allows a child to change his or her future. She was and is, via her founding of Association Montessori Internationale (AMI), the great equalizer. There are many important, successful and proven ways to help children learn. Montessori is not the only way to help children find the knowledge they'll need in this life, but it is certainly one of the most widely proven methods.

CHAPTER TWENTY-THREE

What You Do Matters – Here's Some Proof

We spend a lot of time focused on improving our centers and schools. You have to be driven to be successful in this industry. Whether it's daycare, childcare, preschools, Montessori or private elementary, when you do it right, the impact you create is probably much bigger than you know. Here are some things you should know about your centers and schools:

1. The HighScope Perry Preschool Experiment randomly assigned more than 100 low income, at-risk students to either a two-year preschool program or a control group. The students' lives were reviewed from age three to age 50.

2. Forty-four percent more students graduated high school when they were included in the two-year preschool program.

3. Graduates of the two-year preschool program had income levels that were 36% higher than those who didn't get to attend the program.

4. When we are young children, our collective knowledge is much smaller. So adding the ability to learn makes a greater impact.

5. High-quality early education programs have a positive impact for all racial and economic groups across the country. "Impact" means that we're more likely to have better jobs, be responsible citizens, raise good kids and stay out of prison.

6. There are people who wake up every day and live a life that is far better than the one they should be living. They probably don't know that their life changed because someone like you had the drive to make it possible.

Whether you see yourself as an educator in a business world or a business person selling education, you're providing the best product on planet Earth. Everything…or nothing changes based on access to education.

Winning Daily

CHAPTER TWENTY-FOUR

Early Education – How To Have Productive Meetings

If you're in business, you have meetings. The key is to be focused on the important factors. Otherwise, don't have meetings. They simply add one more thing to your and your staff's already overloaded to-do lists. It's important to meet and manage your center or school proactively. Here are a few ways to be proactive and spend your time and energy more efficiently and effectively:

1. Don't have a standard "every Monday at 9:00 AM" type of meeting. These meetings become routine very quickly. Have meetings because you need to have meetings—not because it's 9:00 AM on a Monday. Set your meetings for different days and different times.

2. If there is not enough work to fill the hour, then don't have a one-hour meeting. These meetings meander and become boring for most everyone who isn't speaking. Meandering and boredom can cause your people to miss the important parts.

3. If you can avoid it, don't have the meeting in the exact same place every time. If you're meeting with your management team, get off the campus and find a private area in a restaurant or some other venue outside of your centers or schools. If you're meeting with your teachers as a group, have snacks, drinks…etc.

4. Pick times during the day when your staff has a high energy level so they are more likely to contribute positively to the meeting—not at the end of the day when some people just want to finish and go home.

5. Make sure to advise staff of the meeting times and places well in advance so they can be prepared.

6. Encourage your staff to bring their own questions and ideas to meetings. There is no reason to think that good ideas can only come from an owner or executive. Your teachers talk with and listen to your parents. The odds of receiving good ideas grow exponentially when you allow others to contribute.

7. Make sure you are the most well-prepared person in the room when you start your meetings. Remember, your staff will follow your lead…good or bad. Never try to "wing it". Have copies of the meeting agenda to help everyone to stay focused.

8. To determine whether you need more, fewer, longer or shorter meetings, review your meeting agenda immediately after your meeting, and determine how much was actually accomplished in the meeting…adjust accordingly.

If you follow these strategies, you'll find that meetings will become more energetic and productive. They will be a source of creativity and problem solving. As strange or unlikely as it may seem to you right now, people will look forward to the meetings, and your company will reap the benefits.

CHAPTER TWENTY-FIVE

Dealing With Change In Your Childcare Company or School

It's said that change is the only constant. In the early education industry, you must change or become irrelevant. How and when you deal with change determines your level of success. If you're comfortable or satisfied, you can coast, but if you want to be really good at anything, you have to push when others choose to relax. This ideology is from the school of "If you're not leading, then you're falling behind."

It's easy to accept thoughts like "That's the way it's always been done" or "If it's not broken, don't fix it". It doesn't matter how it was done or if it's not broken when you're trying to be the best instead of the norm.

Let's talk about how to deal with change so you can avoid the challenges that may occur if you keep the status quo. In order to effectively implement changes you need to hold everyone accountable (including yourself).

Here are three steps you can take to help ensure that your staff will accept and embrace changes:

1. Keep your communication channels open and be sure that everyone understands what is being done and why it is being done. Get key people involved in the process.

2. Have a plan for implementing the change and be able to talk about it in detail. Staff members, like most people, are more willing to follow a smart, strong leader when she's is wrong before they will follow a weak leader when she's right. So if you're smart, strong and right, you should be in good shape.

3. Be flexible. It's rare for anything to go exactly as planned. It's normal for policy to be adjusted over time.

Our industry continues to grow stronger and be more productive. What was once glorified babysitting is now a vital resource for jumpstarting the minds of our youngest people...a tool for putting tomorrow's adults on the right path.

NATURAL DISASTERS AND SCRAMBLING

The weather/natural disaster problems require a little more creativity. We have talked with people whose centers have been flooded or damaged by fire. If the person has multiple locations, then the answer is easy. The children attend one of the other locations until the problem is fixed. If you only have one center and you're faced with losing your enrollment to your competition, then you have to scramble. You can't just find space, you have to find space that is acceptable to parents and licensing.

Note: Have business interruption insurance if you're in an area that's prone to any natural disasters. You have to get equipment into the space quickly. You must comfort your parents so they don't go to and stay with your competition. Sometimes, the answer is as simple as using classroom space already set up in a nearby church. Sometimes, you have to make an alliance with your competition. For example, you agree with your competitor that you will steer your clients to them for a predetermined time period in which they will receive the tuitions (or a portion of) of your clients/parents, but the competitor must agree that they cannot continue to accept your clients after a predetermined date—the date that the flood repairs are completed and approved.

CHAPTER TWENTY-SIX

The Importance of Communication In Your Childcare Company or School

Developing good relationships with your management team, parents, teachers, vendors and your students is a key component to operating a successful center or school. Every aspect of your business – staff satisfaction, parent interaction, teaching the children, managing your staff – comes down to effective communication.

Communication skills are critical to developing and nurturing these essential relationships. You are not working in a widget factory or washing cars. You are caring for and educating people's children. Nothing is more sacred than a person's son or daughter, so any miscommunication, particularly in a potentially stressful moment, can become hypersensitive very quickly.

It's important to be direct and honest with people, but being tactful is also paramount. In any situation where expert communication skills are required, keep your eye on what you want the outcome of the conversation to be. Don't go into any situation where you are addressing a parent, teacher, staff member, or child without knowing what you want to accomplish as a result of the conversation. Again, don't "wing it".

When you talk with any person, make sure you are wholly focused on that person. Don't be looking at your phone...don't let other people interrupt the conversation. When the person is talking, listen closely. Don't just pretend to listen while you're waiting for another opportunity to talk. This task isn't always easy when you're busy, but it is more effective. One focused conversation may save you three repeat conversations.

CHAPTER TWENTY-SEVEN

Mother or Management – What Children and Schools Need

The early education industry is blessed to have many people who enter this business because they care about more than the money. But make no mistake, money is required if you want to stay in this industry. Over the years (especially during a recession), we've seen many people lose schools or pushed to the edge of bankruptcy because they weren't willing to make the necessary decisions associated with good management. Many owners feel that it is their responsibility to take care of ("mother") their teachers. In some cases, they felt guilty. They felt like failures because their school couldn't afford the extra payroll cost, so they spent themselves into deeper debt so their teachers could pay their bills. Incredibly noble…there is nothing like being the hero in somebody's life even when they don't know it, but you must have limits.

The most common and costly mistake we make in this business is the failure to control payroll costs. The second most costly mistake is providing lackluster service because teachers and other employees don't understand or don't care about meeting the expectations of their employer, director or you. Good, honest, hard-working, caring teachers and other staff members deserve the very best career environment possible from the centers and schools that employ them. These are your committed people. These people are your core staff. These are the people that you don't have to worry about much. However, your non-core staff requires more guidance…not mothering guidance. If your non-core staff understands that hours go to the best employees and that you (their boss, not mother) can teach them how to be "best", then you will have the solid platform you need to fix or prevent the two biggest and most costly mistakes in the business.

When you're faced with making that decision between mothering and management, try to remember that running a better, more profitable school allows you to build a bigger business that will serve more children, provide jobs for more teachers and give you and your family the benefits and choices that come with greater financial success. Entrepreneurs and their families sacrifice a lot to create something from nothing. You deserve to keep the rewards you've earned.

Section 2
Growing

Using Tech To Grow

Using Twitter To Market Your Childcare Company

Twitter is the most misunderstood and underutilized platform of all the social media tools we have available to us. Everyone wonders what they could possibly do with Twitter that could benefit their center or school. You can only use 140 characters or less, so there's not much room for a long informative post...and who is going to see it anyway?

Currently, Twitter has 126,000,000 users. It is very low cost marketing, so using this tool becomes profitable quickly. This tool is great for keeping parents engaged by providing pertinent updates on your center's activities. Ask your parents to follow your center or school on Twitter. They will be more connected to you, and your parents may retweet your information to other prospective parents/clients.

Over 75% of people now use a smartphone to manage their daily lives. And even though you can use Twitter on your desktop, laptop, tablet, and other devices, it is an excellent mobile platform. You simply download the app to your smartphone, and you become more nimble in your business practices.

Here are a four ways you can utilize Twitter in your center or school:

1. Set up a private and a public account. The public account will be used for marketing. The private account will be used for protected messaging. Protected messaging would include communicating with parents.

2. It is estimated that Twitter is the #3 or #4 search engine. So take advantage of this technology to see what your competition is doing on Twitter. You can do local searches using hashtags. For example, #childcarecenter [nameofyourcityortown] to search centers in your area or #childcare [center name] to search for a specific center. This will give you ideas about what you could be doing to be more competitive.

3. It's important that you create a sense of community around your center. Twitter can help you with this task. If you are providing updates, relevant educational content, and other useful information about your center through an easy to access platform such as Twitter, you will likely see more involvement and engagement from your parents which could ensure they stay with your center and recommend you to others.

4. Parents sometimes post their desire for good centers and may reach out to their followers on Facebook or Twitter to get references or referrals from other parents who are using a specific center in their area. Remember, the key to marketing is to be in the consciousness of your prospective clients/parents when they are ready to act.

If you are active online and using tools like Twitter to stay engaged with your audience, then you are more likely to reap the rewards for your hard work.

CHAPTER TWENTY-NINE

Why You Need A Website For Your Childcare Company or School

If you are in the early education business, you need a web presence. Having a professionally designed website enhances your brand and gives you credibility in the marketplace for a relatively low cost.

Credibility:

A professionally designed website gives your center or school credibility. Conversely, having a poorly designed website or no website diminishes your company's credibility. In today's world, websites are a requirement for companies interested in growth. When prospective parents are searching for a center or school that meets their needs, the search nearly always starts online. It is rare indeed when anyone grabs a thick yellow book and flips through the pages to find a company these days. Your website helps to ensure that your company is not weeded out when prospects are searching for a company like your company. The look and content of your website can be the difference between becoming irrelevant to that prospective parent and that parent's decision to call you for a tour.

Cost Savings:

Nearly everything that used to require paper and postage can be done from your website. Your forms, contact information, directions to your school, reports to your parents, marketing and promotional materials can all be done from your website for a much lower cost and less labor. You can also personalize your site by having pictures of your center's classrooms and teachers. You can share stories from parents and former students about their positive experiences at your center…all without the materials and distribution cost of paper.

Depending on how your site is set up, you may be able to change the content on your site yourself. Today, most websites are developed in WordPress. Once the site is built, it's very easy to make minor modifications to your site without having to pay a web designer to do everything. You just have to make sure you find a web designer who will work with you and provide a little training on how to do it.

Your website can also save you time. For example, you could have a FAQ (frequently asked questions) section on your website to answer questions that your staff has been answering via phone conversations. While phone conversations are sometimes preferred by you because they help you to deliver more personal service, there is a growing number of people for whom your website provides a more comfortable alternative. It allows them to do their homework anonymously before they call you for the parental tour.

CHAPTER THIRTY

How Do I Use Social Media To Improve My Early Education Company?

Social Media is an extremely inexpensive and useful tool for finding, engaging and retaining clients and staff. In today's world, we go online whenever we want to find or research most anything. Using social media raises your visibility. Parents, teachers and potential business allies look for you online.

It's all about having a presence in a connected world. As human beings, we want to feel comfortable with the people and companies we choose...especially when trusting somebody with our kids. While there are many platforms you can use to connect - Facebook, Twitter, Pinterest, YouTube, LinkedIn and Instagram - you don't have to be able to run NASA or lose sleep to utilize social media.

1. You can use this tool safely in a controlled environment so children and staff members aren't put at risk. So, for example, you could create a Facebook Group so you can monitor and control who joins the group. You can also monitor the interaction on your page to make sure nothing gets posted without your approval. Twitter allows you to create a public

profile for marketing and a private profile just for parents. With a little preparation and the proper setup, you can rest easy knowing privacy won't be an issue.

2. Finding time to devote to social media is the same task you perform for all of the things on your schedule. It's easy to get overwhelmed by all the options. The key is consistency. Spending 30 minutes a day is enough to get results from social media. Remember, you don't have to engage in all the major platforms. If you don't know where to start, ask your parents what social media platforms they like to use.

Social media does take time, but with all of our devices, parents, prospects, teachers and other business people are able to connect with you at their convenience 24/7.

CHAPTER THIRTY-ONE

Why Should I Take The Time To Create A Monthly Newsletter For My Childcare Center or School?

Because, if you do it right, then you will take the time to write the newsletter one time per month, and each newsletter will work for you online 24 hours a day, seven days a week for the next two to three years. So, you're not actually taking time. You are leveraging and saving time. The newsletter gives you the opportunity to show your clients and future clients, that you are smarter, more dedicated and more deserving of their trust and their business.

The primary key is to be pertinent, helpful, honest and direct. If your newsletters have these four attributes, you will stand out from the pack. Anybody can write a pamphlet. Anybody can set another advertisement adrift in a sea of noise. Be different. Don't "write" a newsletter. Use the newsletter to "talk" with your parents. Talk with them the way you wish people would talk with you.

Here's how we start separating you from the crowd. Use professional email marketing. The email marketing I'm referring to involves using a professional email marketing company (Constant Contact is one example) that will not only provide you with the ability to communicate professionally, but also the metrics that will help you measure and determine if and how well your email marketing is working.

The metrics you want to track include opens, bounces, clicks, forwards, spam reports, and opt-outs. A professional email marketing company will make this tracking process easy for you. Remember, if it is truthful feedback, good or bad, then it can be helpful to you.

Here are a few tips for creating your first newsletter:

1. Have someone else review your work before you publish it no matter how good you may be at writing.

2. Use a professional email service provider like Constant Contact. See http://constantcontact.com. It may take a little time to get used to their system, but the system works.

3. Create a professional looking template that carries the brand of your center or school with consistency.

4. Use your logo and other branding materials at the top of your newsletter so the recipients learn to recognize you quickly.

5. Choose topics that are of genuine interest to parents. Avoid picking topics simply because you find it easy to write about them.

6. Keep your newsletter short and to the point. It's not poetry. It's information for making their life better in some way.

7. Be consistent. Monthly is the most common frequency for sending an email newsletter. Pick a day of the month

(for example, the second Tuesday), and publish on that day every month.

8. Use lots of images to draw the reader's attention. While content is most important, it's useless if no one reads it.

9. Create a permission-based list and keep your list current. Your list is an incredibly valuable asset in your business. Collect email addresses so you can stay connected with the people who make it possible for your business to thrive.

If you do these nine things listed above, you will have success with email marketing and increase the chances that your center or school will grow and flourish.

CHAPTER THIRTY-TWO

Using Video To Market Your Childcare Company, Preschool, Montessori School or Private Elementary

Video has become vastly more important as a marketing tool for business—including centers and schools. In 2006, Google bought a two-year-old company called YouTube in a deal worth $1.65 Billion. Video is that important. BFS® and its clients have seen the power of video as a relatively inexpensive tool for gaining the attention of clients, prospective clients and other helpful contacts. Just as important as gaining the attention of others is the ability to use the medium to provide information in an easily understandable format.

Here are three ways you can use video marketing to help your school:

1. Set up a flat screen. Today you see flat screens in businesses ranging from fast food restaurants to the most posh spas and clubs. For as little as $275 per video, you can create a professional video to be looped so it is constantly sending the message that you want to send to anyone who enters your center or school. Depending on the size you choose, a

substantial flat screen TV can be purchased for about the same price as one or two videos, and you have the flexibility to position these flat screens in the areas where you can both educate and entertain your viewers. Your video can discuss anything from new programs coming to your school to a referral program to reward your parents when they refer other parents to your center. As a side benefit, your looped discussion of the exceptional services and activities of your school serves as a constant reminder to your staff. Providing helpful information to the people who need it via video is a great way to separate yourself from the competition without exhausting your advertising budget.

2. Create your own YouTube Channel. Another way to generate buzz from a video marketing campaign is to create a YouTube channel for all your videos. Once established, make sure to email the link to your channel to your parents as this tool is one more item that creates a genuine connection between you and your parents. Additionally, if you and your employees have the link in your email stationery, it makes it very easy to send it to others for their immediate access. We're fortunate to work in an industry of educated people, but you'll also find that many people prefer watching a video to reading an article. Making the learning process easier works for everyone. When you set up your YouTube channel, fill in the "description" underneath the YouTube video. Make your website address the first thing in the description, and then type in a few sentences using keywords that your prospects may type in when searching for a center or school.

3. Maintain access to your videos. If you make sure that you have quick access to your video(s) via all of your devices,

then it becomes second nature to send it to the people you meet…much like a business card but more interesting.

Keep in mind that it is best to invest in a professional quality video. Take some time and make sure your message is authentic. Remember that the video is not about you. It's about the people who want or need the information you possess. Videos score high with the search engines. It is an opportunity to clearly state what makes your school better while you simultaneously improve your SEO (search engine optimization) so you can be found by the major search engines.

CHAPTER THIRTY-THREE

Using Pinterest To Improve Your Early Education Company

Pinterest is a social media platform that allows you to create virtual boards and pin items on the boards. People spend more time on Pinterest that any other social media platform with the exception of Facebook, so it's a great marketing platform. It is also a great way to build brand loyalty by engaging and educating your parents. You can download the Pinterest app to your smartphone or tablet in addition to using it on your computer. If you want to set up an account, go to https://business.pinterest.com/en.

Once you set up an account, you will want to create a few boards. For example, you could create boards for crafts, pictures of your teachers, pictures of your school and a board with pictures of your events like graduation, recitals or fieldtrips. You could also set up a board for parents with topics to help parents with parenting...how to potty train...etc.

The goal is to demonstrate that you are a reliable, knowledgeable resource for anyone interested in interacting with your company. Make sure that anything you post provides real value to parents, teachers, vendors or prospects. Keep in mind that Pinterest is a public platform so be careful to avoid posting anything that could be offensive or a violation of privacy.

An easy way to learn how to use Pinterest is to go to YouTube and watch a couple of videos. Type "how to use Pinterest" in the search bar on YouTube and you will find many resources that will teach you how to use Pinterest correctly.

Pinterest is a great branding tool for your business as it gives you a way to give everyone an inside look at what you are doing in your company and your community. Pinterest is just one more free tool that could give you an edge over your competition.

CHAPTER THIRTY-FOUR

Embracing Technology In Your Early Education Company

When Henry Ford created the first Model T automobile, he was asked about the input he received from other people. His answer was…"If I had asked people what they wanted, they would have said faster horses." The car, like refrigeration, antibiotics, the computer and the smartphone, changed the way our society works. People weren't prepared for the change, but change happened anyway. Like the many people who continued to ride horses as a means of transportation, it's not wrong but ultimately you'll find that others are passing you by.

One of today's "automobiles" is the smartphone. Most of us have a smartphone, but we don't use it to its full advantage. Here are some uses for your smartphone that will help to keep others from passing you by. You can…

1. Review the daily enrollment breakdown when your director sends it to you.

2. Check on your parent connections on any of the social media platforms you use for your company.

3. Check and answer your email.

4. Text with your directors and other employees.

5. Contact vendors during the rush of your day.

6. Instead of long descriptions, take pictures of things that need to be done and send them to the people who need to get them done.

7. Make notes for yourself so your checklists are always with you.

8. Review and update your calendar.

9. Access your bank accounts.

10. Use these devices to have live conversations with other people while not being tethered to a landline.

All of these items can help you to move through your day faster and more productively. You have a super computer in your pocket—not just a phone.

Humans For Growth

CHAPTER THIRTY-FIVE

Connecting With Parents In Your Early Education Company

Relationships are at the core of any successful center or school. This includes the interaction you have with parents, teachers, children and your vendors. Engaging the members of each of these four groups will help to ensure that your school is more successful.

From the first time a parent encounters one of your advertisements to an exit interview when they leave your school, you are engaging that parent with your points of contact. As we work in a competitive environment, it's important to make every contact as beneficial as possible.

Here are a few ways to connect with your parents:

1. Internet Presence. For many early education companies, this one is limited to a website, and many times these websites are created, launched and forgotten. Your website gives you the opportunity to provide parents with the best and most up-to-date information about your school and its activities. It gives you the chance to show parents that you are better and more knowledgeable than your competition. Review and improve

your website at least every 90 days. It may only be small changes in the beginning, but getting in the habit will lead you to learn more and make bigger improvements as you move forward.

2. Social Media Platforms. Facebook, Twitter, Pinterest, LinkedIn, YouTube and Instagram are all useful platforms.

3. Staff. Every staff member, from your director and teachers to your cook and maintenance person, can be a walking ambassador for your company. Who knows more than these people about the way "their" school performs? Everyone spends money on advertising. If you choose to incentivize your staff for bringing more parents in the door, you have the opportunity to increase your enrollment and reward your staff…creating greater staff loyalty as a byproduct. While it may not be typical for you, advertising expense paid to staff can certainly be more beneficial for you than the money you spend with vendors.

4. Vendors. Most people don't think of their vendors as sources of new business, but your vendors very likely interact with many parents in your local area. These people are highly rated and often overlooked resources. These relationships can be set up as barter relationships (they send parents to you and you send clients to them) or you can choose to pay them for each new referral that stays enrolled for X period of time. No matter how you do it, these people know people…including their own children.

5. Print Media. While print media is used less in the age of the Internet and social media connectivity, it is still an important factor for getting the initial attention of parents and for

keeping parents informed once they have become clients. There is still a solid place for print media. While digital media is faster and cheaper, it doesn't cover everything.

6. The Exit Interview. If you conduct exit interviews with your staff or parents, you have the opportunity to learn how you can better connect with parents. Many people will share information in an exit interview that they won't share in the middle of a relationship. This is a great way to discover new options.

7. Local Elementary Schools. There are few things better than teachers from local schools that will recommend your center or school to a parent. These contact points can send elementary age children to you as well as their younger siblings.

8. Open House. An open house for local parents to view your school and meet your teachers is always fun and not terribly expensive for the opportunity to be face to face with potential clients.

These proven tools can greatly improve your early education company. Their effective use can also provide you with a compounding effect as more parents who become clients become referral sources for you as well.

CHAPTER THIRTY-SIX

Expanding Your Early Education Company

OK, you're on your way. Your SOPs are in order and you're ready to do everything bigger and better. That is great, but do it the right way. The bankruptcy dockets are full of companies that were expanding.

When you consider expansion, make sure you have the basics in order before you start investing your time and money. Here are the basics:

1. SOPs - If you don't have a well-organized set of SOPs (standard operating procedures), then you need to start here. These SOPs are important for the operation of your current locations as well as future locations. You may think that you've got it covered without a good set of SOPs, but when you see the difference in your company with SOPs, you'll understand why they are so important. When your company is small enough for you to keep your finger on the pulse of every center, that's one thing. However, to really grow you have to have a mechanism/procedures that provide an easily and clearly understood course of action for every event.

2. How To Expand - You'll need to decide how you want to expand. Do you want to build new facilities? Do you want to buy operating centers or schools? Do you want to buy your competition? Do you want to buy struggling centers for less money and fix them? Do you want to buy schools at the top of their game? Do you want to diversify the demographic you currently serve? Do you want to diversify so you aren't so dependent upon a large employer in your area? These questions are just the starting point, and every question is important.

3. Business Plan - Have a well-organized business plan for yourself and the bankers, investment bankers, private equity firms or family offices that will likely fund your expansion.

4. Financing - Get pre-qualified for the financing you'll need. It's not difficult if you work with people who know what they're doing. At the most basic level, try to avoid the resident 12-year-old banker sitting at the lobby desk. He's probably a good, smart kid, but you need experience—not someone who is filling out an application for you.

5. Labor Market - Know your labor market. Finding good teachers and directors is always a challenge. Make sure you have access to these people, especially if you are considering building facilities from the ground up.

6. Economic Changes - When everything is going well, it is very easy to feel like everything will continue to go well. Make sure you are measured and deliberate in your expansion plans. Make sure you can make the necessary adjustments if your expansion gets caught by an economic downturn. It's not dif-

ficult to do when you plan ahead. It can be very difficult to do when you're caught by surprise.

7. **Professional Help** - Engage your CPA, attorney and other necessary professionals in your planning process. Determine if your CPA and attorney have experience in these matters. A good team is always better than a good leader.

CHAPTER THIRTY-SEVEN

Promoting Your Teachers and Your School Through Curriculum and Confidence

When parents visit your center or school, they want to be confident that the teachers in your school are providing an interesting learning environment. For a parent, leaving their child at "school" is far better than leaving their child at a "care" facility. It gives more meaning and purpose to the child's time with you.

That's one of the reasons why it is important to choose or create a curriculum that you and your teachers can present confidently. Whether you're using Creative Curriculum, Teddy Care, Reggio Emilia, Montessori or any number of other choices, you must believe in your choice. If you don't, your teachers won't, and your parents will sense the lack of commitment.

Once you have made a commitment to your curriculum, it's important that you communicate the unique backgrounds, teaching styles, experience, and education levels of your teachers. With today's instant access to information, parents will do more than run a search on your center or school. They will run a search on most anyone that can affect their child's day. The children that you educate and care for probably spend more conscious hours with you and your teachers than with his or her parents. It's understandable that the parent will check out everything about you and your teachers.

Here are a few things you can do to make sure parents find the information they need to know about your teachers:

1. Provide information about each of your teachers on your website. Keep it around 350 – 400 words per teacher. Be sure to avoid sharing any private information. It's ideal to have the teachers draft their own bios, but reserve the option to edit the draft. Regardless, get written approval from each of your teachers before sharing the final draft of the information.

2. Have an open house and introduce all the teachers to your visiting parents. A face to face meeting, preceded or followed by the parent's visit to your website where teachers' pictures and bios are on display, will help parents become more comfortable with your teachers faster.

3. Make sure your teachers can talk about themselves and their work. This activity will help teachers organize their thoughts about themselves, and they will be more comfortable and polished when talking with parents.

Doing these three things correctly can make a huge difference in how your center or school is perceived. If your teacher seems average, then the parent may or may not enroll their child. If your teacher is impressive, they are far more likely to enroll their child, AND they will be far more likely to talk about the child's teacher. For your purpose, talking about the great teacher is almost synonymous with talking about the great school. Make sure parents see the reason you hired them.

CHAPTER THIRTY-EIGHT

How Do I Increase Enrollment In My Childcare Center or School?

There are many ways to increase enrollment. Every school and its local market area are unique to a degree so some methods work better than others pending your exact circumstances.

Here are a few methods that have worked successfully:

1. Find and utilize a good SEO (Search Engine Optimization) and social media person. It's no secret that we use search engines to tell us about everything now. A good SEO person will make sure you rank well in the major search engines.

2. Offer referral incentives to your teachers and other staff members as well as your parents. Most of us remember to offer incentives to our parents, but we overlook the ambassadors working in the school every day. Most teachers deserve more pay. This strategy allows you to increase teacher and other staff compensation while improving your profitability.

3. Make friends with the teachers and administrators in your local elementary schools. This is a place where parents will ask about good centers and schools.

4. Many centers do not accept infants. If you're properly licensed, accept infants. Make sure you charge a profitable price. Some centers find it difficult to do so, but many times you can make smaller profits in the infant category and much better profits from their siblings. This also keeps parents from choosing other centers because they don't want to take their children to two different centers.

5. Ask your parents for reference letters—not a thesis, just a simple note with their email address or phone number. This is a very simplistic and direct approach to gaining the trust of prospective new clients. Your parents are typically very happy with your center. If they weren't happy, they would go somewhere else. Make these reference letters a part of the standard package that you give to all new parents/prospective clients. Remember, every center or school your prospective parent visits all say the same thing— "We're the best." If your parents/clients are happy with your performance, then it is very reassuring to tell a prospective parent that you can talk about your own school all day long, but you feel it may be more helpful for them to see what other parents think of your center or school.

6. Next is 4 x 6 postcards. I know. This is old school. Most of us know that direct mail usually generates a return of one percent or less. The key is to make this tool so inexpensive to use that it's worth it to get the one percent. A 4 x 6 postcard is an ideal size because they fit easily into free spaces ranging from a windshield wiper to the countertops and bulletin

boards in local area schools, businesses and the laundry rooms in apartment complexes.

DISCRETION

Regardless of the topic or service, most people worry that someone will find out that they are talking with BFS® or another consulting firm. The assumption is that talking with a consultant means that something is wrong. There are many times when nothing is wrong. We're just working on making the company better. If the company is making $200,000 a year, then we're looking for ways to push it to $250,000 or $300,000. Regardless, our client or prospective client conversations and the work we do for these people is managed with exceptional discretion starting with the first word of the first conversation. In more than 25 years in business, no BFS® client has ever suffered any loss caused by a lack of discretion. If you want to be more careful, have the consultant sign a Non-Disclosure Agreement before talking with them. Reputable, professional firms have no problem with this practice.

CHAPTER THIRTY-NINE

Why Parents and Teachers Love Montessori

There are about 4,000 private, certified Montessori Schools in the U.S. If you talk with anyone who believes in the teachings of Dr. Maria Montessori, you will quickly understand that this person believes without reservation that Montessori is the greatest teaching/learning method ever devised. This desire to believe in an ideal, nearly universal educational learning method, is understandable and especially important in light of the routinely dismal results being produced in most of our public school systems.

The first and most important accomplishment of Montessori is that it recognizes the obvious—Children learn in different ways and at different speeds. This certainly shouldn't be a surprise to anyone today or 100 years ago in the early years of Montessori learning. While much of our public school system operates like an assembly line, there are a handful of these very special places where children get a start that can be no less than the lottery ticket of early education. I am not suggesting that children can't get a great education without Montessori; however and regardless of the source, a child that enters elementary school with confidence and the enjoyment of learning will be miles ahead of the masses.

The second major accomplishment of Montessori is the creation of an environment that nurtures a child so that child has the greatest odds of success in school and in the world beyond school. While Montessori sets boundaries for children, it allows a child to make conscious decisions about what will be learned. The child is driven by personal curiosity instead of the perfunctory rigors of repetition. Children become seekers of information instead of just the processors. When a child makes a mistake, he can review and learn from the mistake in an environment where mistakes aren't wrong. Mistakes are just a very normal part of the learning process.

When a child enters the relatively large classroom of a public school, there are many factors that interrupt the learning process. Many children without the necessary attention early in the education process will be lost to these distractions. Children can and do get through the entire public school system from first grade through high school graduation without ever reading an entire book and without learning to think all while receiving As and Bs. It happens. When a child learns how to learn instead of learning how to regurgitate memorized answers, everything becomes possible. The teaching methods, materials and environments utilized in the Montessori process are tools that teach children how to think and by extension how to become better and more fulfilled human beings.

Section 3
Selling

Timing Your Sale

How Long Does It Take To Sell An Early Education Company?

If you talk with enough brokerage companies, you will likely receive every answer from three weeks (not true) to a year. The amount of time it takes to actually sell your early education company varies from 120 days to a year…and occasionally it takes more than a year.

The amount of time is directly related to nine factors that can be affected by the seller or seller's representatives. The factors are as follows:

1. **Brokerage Firm** - Choose the right one as a professional brokerage firm organizes and coordinates the other professionals involved in the sales transaction. The professionals include the buyers, attorneys, appraisers, inspectors, CPAs, financing sources, SBA personnel, and licensing representatives. It's extremely important that your brokerage firm knows what everyone should do, when they should do it and how to coordinate these professionals.

2. **Buyers** - Make sure they are always qualified financially and educationally. Many potential buyers will not survive the

rigors of the due diligence, financing and licensing processes on the way to closing a transaction. It is important to pre-qualify buyers correctly. No one wants to work on a deal that fails.

3. Lenders - Make sure that buyers have dependable lenders. From private equity firms to credit unions, sellers and buyers need to know more than the lender is capable and willing. Know that the lender understands the early education industry and makes loans for the acquisition of companies in this specific industry.

4. Attorneys - Hire the right type of attorney. Attorneys typically focus on an area of expertise. Your attorney may be the best patent attorney in the world, but that doesn't make him the right person to guide you through the legal rigors of your transaction.

5. Accountant/CPA - At some point in your transaction (assuming it is handled properly) you are going to be asked the following question: How do you want to accept the money? Make sure your CPA is prepared to answer the question with the best possible option for you specifically. Remember, the only part of the money that counts for you and your family is the part you get to keep.

6. Loan Document Organizers - Whether the function is fulfilled by a bank or a mortgage broker, make sure they have a track record for managing loans that close. Any company can accept fees and get half way through the process. Don't be afraid to ask about a track record. It could save you fees, time, energy and frustration.

7. Licensing Process - If your transaction is going to close, then it must be blessed by state licensing. Given the need for discretion in our industry, it is imperative to be well-prepared for this conversation as well as the timing of the conversation.

8. Closing - Always have the closing managed by a professional law firm, title company or escrow company. It isn't very expensive, and it helps ensure that nothing is overlooked.

9. Transition - Many people are so focused on getting through closing that they forget the importance of transitioning the centers or schools smoothly to the new owners. When a transaction is managed properly, buyers and sellers will be well-organized. Template documents will be provided to buyer and seller so the transition is as comfortable as possible for the seller, buyer, staff and parents of the centers or schools involved.

CHAPTER FORTY-ONE

Market Timing In The Early Education Industry

In every industry and economic cycle, there are always people who believe that they can predict the future usually because they have some business model that's been right at least once. This authority will point to their example of being right without discussing how many times they have been wrong and explain that you're safe if you trust them. From investment banking to preschools, it has been my experience that very few people have this gift and most business models built to predict the future are fatally flawed somewhere, usually in the assumptions made about the very foundation of the model.

I know a lot of financially successful people, and one of the things that most all of them agree on is that economist and other various professionals who predict the future are wrong far more than they're right. We have a wonderfully resilient industry, but it has its weaknesses too.

One of the things we learned in the "great" recession is that loss of jobs, falling real estate values, too much consumer debt and/or failures of banks to lend within our industry will cause many sleepless nights…or worse. It's rare that anyone calls the exact timing of any major change in economic trends.

The seller with profits has the golden ticket. No one can tell you when the time is right for you to sell or not sell your early education company. However, as time and experience has taught many of us, going out on top means paying attention to what <u>could</u> happen and evaluating the likelihood of those risks.

NO NEED TO KEEP YOUR GUARD UP

I always enjoy that moment in a new relationship with a client or prospective client when they realize that they don't need to be guarded with us. Oftentimes, these people have had poor experiences with other brokerage firms or business in general. You can feel their intensity when you're on the phone. They're just waiting for the big sales pitch...the place where the broker tries to trick them into something by lying about their track record or faking knowledge of the industry. I want to help them alleviate that stress point as soon as possible, but all you can really do is give them verifiable information and time to get comfortable with it. The best of these moments are the prospective clients that do a deep dive into BFS®. Sometimes they'll hire their law firm to do the work. At the end of the day, they typically come back to us more relaxed and ready to work together.

CHAPTER FORTY-TWO

How Do I Know When It's Time To Sell My Early Education Company?

We get this question in one form or another most every day. The short answer is that you should sell whenever you want to sell. However, your decision to sell (or not sell) is oftentimes shaped by a number of factors. If you recognize these factors and their effect on your decision-making process, then you'll be better equipped to make the best decision for you. Here are a few things to consider when deciding whether or not to sell your early education company:

1. Life Timing - Some of our clients talk with us off and on for years before they decide to sell. Whenever you decide to sell, it's best to sell from a position of strength. Too often, people begin to get tired and the performance of their centers or schools slowly declines. It's like a pro athlete at the end of a sports career. However, unlike the pro athlete, the largest payday in your early education career is most often the last day of your career, so it's important to protect it.

2. Economic Timing - As many people learned in the 2008+ real estate collapse and the stock market crash, you can do everything right and still lose...in some cases lose

everything. Some of our most grateful clients are the people who sold in 2007. Whether they were watching the economy or just lucky, the difference in selling in a good market versus a bad one can mean a swing of 60% or more in the value of your early education company.

3. **Health** - Your and your family's health has a strong influence on your ability to manage or oversee the quality of your program. While most of us will push ourselves much harder to care for the people who mean the most to us, there are mental and physical limits for everyone. Make sure to pay attention to these limits. Sometimes, you and your family will do better to take the bigger payday earlier than planned.

4. **Retirement** - As you approach retirement, it's a good idea to reduce the amount of risk in your portfolio. Whether your portfolio contains stocks, bonds, options, real estate, art or a collection of companies, you don't want to get caught in a high-risk position when you don't have as many years to recoup losses.

5. **New Challenges** - Many people become very successful in the early education industry. Once everything is well-organized and the company requires less of the owner's time, many entrepreneurs look for new opportunities. Some people manage to oversee the operations of their early education company successfully after adding a new company, and some early education companies suffer when the owner is distracted by other pursuits. It's important to know the capacity of your-self and your management team when you begin to step out of the daily operations.

From a purely business perspective, the goal is to always maximize your return on investment. By paying attention to these five primary factors, you will increase your odds of maximizing your financial returns.

How To Get The Most

How To Get The Best Appraisal For Your Early Education Real Estate At The Best Price

Getting the best real estate appraisal for your real estate is a function of four things:

1. Knowing the type of appraisal you need.

2. Hiring the right appraiser.

3. Reviewing the appraisal.

4. Researching and asking the right questions of your appraiser.

First, not all appraisals have the same purpose or cost so it's important to tell the appraiser exactly what you need from him. If you simply ask for "an appraisal", then you can receive bids that may range from a $1,000 to more than $12,000 for a single property. In this circumstance, you are looking for an appraisal that tells you the value for your land and building(s) only. This type of appraisal is commonly referred to as a "Bricks and Mortar" appraisal (also called a Limited Use or Restricted Use Appraisal). All markets are different, but this type of appraisal will usually cost between $1,500 and $2,500 and it will tell you the current market value of your land and building(s) only—not the value of your business component.

Second, hiring the right appraiser means knowing that all appraisers are not the same. When given the opportunity, try to hire appraisers who are "MAI" qualified. While the MAI designation isn't required to get a professional appraisal, appraisers with this designation tend to be better qualified for the work. When you are interviewing appraisers, ask them if they typically do all of their work for banks. It's not always true, but many appraisers who work exclusively for banks tend to provide appraisals that are less focused on maximizing the market value of properties and more focused on collateralizing the bank loan amounts of those properties. Given a choice, I recommend qualified real estate appraisers who don't work exclusively for banks.

Third, many people receive the appraisal they buy and accept the appraisal as perfect. Many times they are perfect. However, it is a good practice to review the appraisal and see if the appraiser used the best comps available for your property—not just an acceptable number of comps. General information on similar properties sold in your area can be accessed via the Internet or a friendly local real estate broker.

Fourth, if you find information that you feel should have been used in your appraisal, contact your appraiser as quickly as possible and ask him or her to revise the appraisal accordingly. As long as the new information is applicable to your property, the appraiser will normally revise the appraisal at no cost to you. Remember, whether the increase in the appraised value of your property is $5,000 or $50,000, it will be value earned with a relatively small amount of effort on your part.

CHAPTER FORTY-FOUR

Is My Multi-Unit Early Education Company Worth More If I Sell Multiple Centers Simultaneously?

The answer is yes, as long as the majority of your company profits don't come from just one of your locations. The closing sales price can be as much as 60% higher for a small chain of centers or schools when compared to the sales price for selling a one or two school company. This math is not the lottery version of selling centers and schools. This is a very normal, realistic practice. For clarity, we are not talking about related real estate. We are only talking about the business components.

Here are some of the pertinent factors:

1. Buying multiple centers from one selling company: This scenario is the favorite for buyers. This enables the buyer to review the financials for only one company and acquire multiple locations. For example, when a buyer buys a chain of five centers, they only have to complete due diligence for one acquisition. If they purchase five centers one center at a time, then it is approximately five times more work for the same results. The buyer also suffers higher costs as attorneys,

CPAs, real estate appraisers, Phase 1 inspectors…etc. have to be paid for each transaction. While the cost ratio isn't a perfect five to one, transactional costs are definitely less for a buyer that purchases a well-organized chain than a buyer that buys five single center companies.

2. Buying multiple centers simultaneously from multiple selling companies: This scenario is the second favorite for most buyers. It requires more effort and cost on the part of the buyer, but it still allows the buyer to save time and money. Extending from the example in #1, buyers would rather buy five centers from two selling companies than from five selling companies for the same reasons discussed in #1. However, this dynamic can cause transaction closings to be delayed significantly. Sales that are supposed to close 90 days after the LOI (Letter of Intent) is signed can stretch to a year or more if the transaction isn't properly managed. We've heard the horror stories over the last 25 years, and the only thing that's worse than a transaction that takes a year to close is a transaction that takes a year and doesn't close. Generally speaking, anything that causes a seller's transaction to stretch out (including waiting for due diligence on another seller's company) is usually not good for the seller. Conversely, many transactions are completed this way, and this scenario or structure can be better for everyone involved. The BFS® team has completed many "roll-ups" over the years. However, we never allow the purchase of a client's center(s) to be delayed for a buyer's roll-up. Strong, professional buyers don't have to delay for a roll-up. The key for buyers is to have a well-organized, focused acquisition team and dependable financing. Note: Many buyers say they can close quickly for all cash particularly when multiple centers are available. There is every reason to believe that buyers do want to close quickly

and that they will pay you all cash at closing, but desire or passion without focus and ability usually leads to frustration. It is very important to know your buyer's qualifications and track record for closing deals.

3. Timing a transaction. Timing can be absolutely crucial. Here are a few timing factors that can influence the results of your transaction:

    a. Is the buyer changing financing sources? Whether the buyer utilizes funds from a bank, investment bank, private equity fund, a REIT or a rich uncle, whenever the source of funds changes in the middle of a transaction, you face the risk that the new source of funds won't like the buyer's transaction with you.

    b. If the buyer is a smaller company, have they made any recent acquisitions or divestitures? Are they working through the changes related to a recent purchase? Have they sold anything that improved their cash position or reduced their outstanding debt?

    c. Do they already have other centers in your area? Are they simply enlarging their local market share or are they trying to establish a new market? The tenacity for and the value of a transaction comes from the motivational source.

    d. Are your competitors trying to sell to the same buyer?

    e. How many acquisitions is the buyer attempting at the same time as your transaction? Do they have the necessary bandwidth?

f. Is the buyer trying to close the transaction by the end of their company's fiscal year so they can utilize the tax advantages?

4. Size of your company. All buyers do not work from the same set of acquisition parameters, and each will likely have parameters other than the size of your company (profitability, regional location, their infrastructure, their regional management resources, your management team…etc.) that will affect their level of interest in your company. However, with all else equal, the market value of early education companies (business components—not real estate) will typically show material increases when a selling company has at least one of the following characteristics:

a. More than $3,000,000 in annual revenues.

b. More than $5,000,000 in annual revenues.

c. More than $10,000,000 in annual revenues.

d. More than $500,000 in EBITDA (Earnings Before Interest Taxes Depreciation and Amortization).

e. More than $1,000,000 in EBITDA.

f. More than $5,000,000 in EBITDA.

So, above some minimum targets, selling multiple centers will normally get you a materially higher return on investment; however, it is important to recognize and manage the right factors at the right time.

REPEAT CLIENTS

There are some clients that work with us multiple times. Sometimes they own a chain of centers, and they want to sell off one or two at a time as they move into retirement. These relationships are great. Our client will call out of the blue one day and say...I need you to sell two more this year. Our agreement goes back and forth. Then in a few days, we're off and running. No issues...the client knows us...here's two more...sell them. It's great to have business relationships with that kind of comfort level.

CHAPTER FORTY-FIVE

Sale and Leaseback Transactions

Sale and Leaseback transactions (SLB) can give you more investment cash, higher profits, less debt and allow you to continue operating your early education company without interruption.

These transactions are as simple as they sound. You sell your real estate (not your business) for full market value to a company and simultaneously lease it back from that company. This action can give you less debt, less pressure and the ability to continue making money (oftentimes with higher margins) in your early education business.

The key to a successful SLB is to make sure you get two things:

1. A fair sales price for your real estate. The best way to determine the market value for your real estate is to hire a well-qualified, properly licensed real estate appraiser, and use the procedure we discussed in Chapter 43.

2. The necessary lease terms to maintain or improve your profits. Like every property, every lease is different but you'll want to scrutinize the following factors specifically:

a. Base Rent.

b. Incremental increases in rent including how the increases are stated in the lease. The right wording can provide tax benefits.

c. Common Area Maintenance ("CAM") charges.

d. Property taxes.

e. Property insurance.

f. Repairs and Maintenance.

In the early education industry, "triple net" (or "NNN") leases are the most common. In a triple net lease, the tenant pays the rent plus items D, E and F from the list. Anything can be modified, so don't hesitate to ask questions. For example, you might say yes to paying for Repairs and Maintenance expense but exclude any costs for repairs to the roof or the heating and cooling systems.

Everything is negotiable.

WHY SHOULD I CHOOSE BFS®...ASK ANYBODY

I regularly get the question...Why should we choose BFS® over other consultants? I'm happy to answer the question in as much detail as the person wants, but my favorite answer is to simply tell the person that it's really better if you talk with the people who do business with us. We'll typically send the person 40 or 50 reference letters from our clients including their contact information and suggest that they talk with our clients...Talk with the Better Business Bureau...Talk with the Consumer Protection Agency. No matter who you talk with, you're not going to get anything but good reports about our firm. Anybody that knows anything about us knows that we do exactly what we say we'll do...black and white - no gray.

CHAPTER FORTY-SIX

What To Do With Used Furniture, Fixtures and Equipment (FF&E)

Always talk with an accountant or CPA before deciding the best way to send used FF&E to its next life. Used equipment can certainly be sold online via the usual and well-known vendors, but it can also be donated to other schools or centers in need, orphanages, foster homes, local parks and recreation centers. Donors may receive tax benefits from these donations made to charitable organizations.

For larger equipment that doesn't easily transition to smaller venues, it can be evaluated/appraised and sold to other companies. FF&E valuations from the free rough estimates to detailed reports are provided by BFS® for playground equipment, cribs, cubbies, kitchen equipment, buses, vans, cots, children's furniture, changing stations, beds and more than 200 other items found in centers and schools nationwide.

Sometimes this equipment is simply discarded without regard to its remaining useful life. Unless the equipment is unsafe, there are always children and organizations who want access to this equipment, and it's not hard to find someone who will take it.

Section 4
Buying

All About The Benjamins

CHAPTER FORTY-SEVEN

Choosing The Right Bank

In this industry and this era, there really is no choosing the right bank or the right banker over the long-term. If you want the best results for you and your business, then choose banks and bankers on a case-by-case basis. There are a lot of exceptionally good people who work in banks. However, virtually none of these people make policy decisions. None of these people unilaterally decide if you get your loan and on what terms. Banks have loan portfolios to balance and protect. Banks change the types of loans they make and people and industries they lend to based on the needs of their portfolio and the broader exposures of their bank…and that's the way it should be. The banks lookout for themselves, just as you need to lookout for yourself. While advertising about "relationship" banking is warm and fuzzy, the warm and fuzzy part is usually more for the bank than you. Advertising executives in nice offices in beautiful skyscrapers work very hard on the warm and fuzzy campaigns so it's important for you to make your decisions objectively.

The primary tool for protecting consumer interest has always been a competitive market place. No one works harder when they don't have to compete. Hence, when you're looking for a bank (or any other vendor), make sure the bank understands that they have competition.

Now, here's the good news. Having a long-term banking relationship and making banks compete for your business are not mutually exclusive conditions. Your bank becomes your bank by winning your business the first time. That bank continues to be your bank when they continue to outperform their competition. For example, a bank sells you a home mortgage ("gives you a loan for your house"). They have the best terms, and that's great. They have earned the chance to get the first call when you need a business loan, car loan, credit card...etc. The minute the bank thinks they earned the "only" call instead of the "first" is when you'll start losing ground.

A good bank and a good banker can prove to be very valuable to you and your early education company, but the bank is not your friend or your business partner. They are a vendor. Make them compete to ensure your best interests.

CHANGING THE INDUSTRY - MORE BUYERS AND MORE BANKS

When BFS® and Barnett Real Estate Services, Inc. (BRESI) began there were really just a handful of brokers that were handling most of the business, and no one that I would classify as a strong, national, independent consulting firm. The brokers were all men and most of them were former employees of some the largest childcare companies of the day. They said they represented the seller, but from the reports we received it looked very much like they were signing selling clients and just taking them back to their former friends and colleagues in the major companies. This realization is part of what led me to start BFS® and BRESI. You look at a circumstance and you say...If that's the best they've got, we can do it better. BFS®/BRESI now have more than 5,000 actively engaged buyers...the most competitive bidding environment in the industry today.

It was also true that many of the larger childcare companies took the negotiating position that they were the only ones with money so sellers would need to accept less money for their companies and they would also need to provide seller financing instead of getting all cash at closing. It's not that way today. BFS® related banks routinely finance deals (business and real estate) with 10% down. That means a qualified buyer with $200,000 is just as good as a buyer with $2,000,000 in cash. With many major banks available to us at any time, every qualified buyer can be a cash buyer.

CHAPTER FORTY-EIGHT

How Much Down Payment Money Do I Need To Buy An Early Education Company?

Unfortunately, the answer to this question is one that many people learn the hard way. We can make it easier for you here. The amount of down payment required for your purchase of a childcare center or school is determined primarily by the following factors:

1. Your credit score. Your credit score in this market needs to be 700 or better. In some cases, your score can be in the 600s as long as there is a good reason for it, but ideally you and any partners need to have scores that will average out around 700 or more.

2. Your net worth. The lender in any transaction is looking to gather as much security as possible to ensure that they will be repaid as agreed in the loan documents. This is why banks sometimes look to your assets (collateral) outside of the deal assets. Keep this bank goal in mind when negotiating your terms. Make sure you provide only as much collateral as you choose. Don't let the bank make that choice for you.

185

3. Your occupational background. To manage their risk, the lender will look for you to have previous or related experience in the industry. If you don't have this experience, the bank will look to other areas to mitigate risk.

4. Whether your transaction includes the purchase of real estate with the business. Typically, banks consider real estate to be a better type collateral so stronger real estate values increase banker confidence in the loan.

5. The quality of earnings (QofE) for the selling business. The QofE shows the strength or ability of the company being acquired to repay the loan. The bank is looking at post-closing EBITDA or Free Cash Flow to assess this risk factor.

6. The lender you choose to make the loan. Again, making the banks compete for your loan and knowing what terms to negotiate in your loan play major parts in ensuring your success in this negotiation.

7. Whether the loan is a Conventional or SBA loan. When people think of loans, they usually think of a Conventional loan. This is a loan that is created and agreed to by you and the bank. If the loan is not repaid in full, then it is the bank that suffers the loss...we're assuming the bank didn't sell your loan after closing. In a SBA (Small Business Administration) loan, the SBA will typically guarantee somewhere between 70% and 90% of the loan. So if the SBA loan isn't repaid then the SBA and the bank share in the loss. Hence, the bank has a lower risk factor when you choose to take out a SBA loan.

While there are certainly other factors that will affect the approval of your loan, covering these items successfully will take you most of the distance.

CHAPTER FORTY-NINE

SBA Fees Explained

To offset the costs of its loan programs to the taxpayer, the SBA charges a guaranty fee and a servicing fee for each loan approved and disbursed. The amount of the fees is based on the portion of the loan guaranteed by the SBA. The lender may charge the upfront guaranty fee to the borrower only after the lender has paid the fee to SBA and has made the first disbursement of the loan to you (the borrower). The lender's annual service fee to the SBA cannot be charged to the borrower. For loans approved on or after December 8, 2004, the following fee structure applies:

1. For loans of $150,000 or less, a 2.0% guaranty fee will be charged. Lenders are permitted to retain 0.25% of the upfront guaranty fee on loans with a gross amount of $150,000 or less.

2. For loans of more than $150,000 up to and including $700,000, a 3% guaranty fee will be charged.

3. For loans greater than $700,000, a 3.5% guaranty fee will be charged.

4. For loans greater than $1,000,000, an additional 0.25% guaranty fee will be charged for that portion greater than $1,000,000. The portion of $1,000,000 or less would be charged a 3.5% guaranty fee; the portion greater than $1,000,000 would be charged at 3.75%.

NOTE: The American Recovery and Reinvestment Act signed into law February 17, 2009, authorized the temporary elimination of the borrower upfront guaranty fee on 7(a) loans having a maturity of longer than 12 months, through the end of March 2010, or until the funds appropriated for this provision are exhausted, whichever comes first.

CHAPTER FIFTY

Should I Use Conventional or SBA Financing?

The answer to this question isn't right or wrong. It is a matter of what is better for you. "Conventional" financing is typically defined as a bank loan that is not guaranteed by the SBA. While terms are always negotiable with lending institutions, the primary advantage of using this type of financing is that it allows you to avoid paying SBA fees. Hence, the question becomes…Is it worth the fees to get an SBA loan instead of a conventional loan? While the SBA offers several programs, the two most popular are the "504 Program" and the "7(a) Program". Here are some of the benefits for both programs:

SBA 504 Program:

1. Ninety percent (90%) financing of the total project costs are available for commercial real estate purchases. Using the 504 allows business owners to keep more in cash reserves and creates the opportunity to make a higher cash-on-cash return.

2. Longer loan amortizations allow for smaller monthly payments. Additionally, prepayments are allowed (generally up to 20% of the principal balance during the first ten years),

so business owners can have the best of both worlds — smaller monthly payments for when cash flow is tight and the ability to pay down debt when excess cash allows it. Maximum loan amortization is 25 years for real estate.

3. When properly structured, owning commercial real estate instead of leasing can (doesn't guarantee) give you more control over your annual occupancy costs. Once the mortgage cost is covered, you can adjust your "rent expense" to fit your needs more closely.

4. Financing closing and other soft costs with a 504 loan helps reduce out-of-pocket expenses when business owners make the decision to purchase commercial property and only want to spend the minimum amount of cash necessary.

5. The lack of balloon payments, calls or negative loan covenants enable borrowers to enjoy control and peace of mind with less lender micromanagement.

6. When well-organized, borrowers and lenders can close in 90 days or less allowing the business owner to take possession of their new property as soon as possible.

7. When dealing with a genuine specialist in 504 financing, the experience of buying commercial property can be simple and far less stressful than working with non-specialists. Some specialists can provide twenty-four hour preapprovals and four-day commitments once they receive the necessary information from the borrower.

8. Future sales of properties financed by 504 loans are sometimes benefited by having assumable mortgages.

SBA 7(a) Program:

1. The 7(a) program can be used to secure loans for expansion, renovation, construction of a new facility, purchase of land or buildings, purchase of equipment, fixtures, or leasehold improvements, working capital, refinancing debt for compelling reasons, a seasonal line of credit, acquiring inventory or any legal business expense. For many borrowers, these loans are harder to secure when the bank does not have the SBA guaranty for the loan.

2. The 7(a) can provide a maximum guarantee of $750,000 or 75% of the total loan, whichever is less.

3. For loans of less than $100,000, the guarantee is normally 80%.

4. The guarantee is used to encourage lenders that might not otherwise make the loan. The SBA guaranty assures the lender that if the borrower does not repay the loan, the government will reimburse the lender for its loss, up to the percentage of SBA's guaranty. Note that the borrower still remains responsible for repaying the full outstanding amount of the loan.

5. The specific terms of SBA loans are negotiated between the borrower and the participating lender subject to the requirements of SBA.

6. 7(a) loans have a maximum loan amount of $2 million.

7. Interest rates are negotiated between the borrower and the lender but are subject to SBA maximums which are pegged to

the prime rate, the LIBOR rate or an optional peg rate. Interest rates may be fixed or variable.

CHAPTER FIFTY-ONE

SBA Makes Money Easier With Lending Parameters

If you think borrowing money was easy before, now it's cheap and more plentiful. Effective January 2018, the SBA has made a major adjustment to their basic acquisition lending parameters.

Here's how it changed.

In recent history, the SBA has required a minimum of a 25% down payment on the purchase of businesses and a 10% down payment on the purchase of the real estate that often comes with these businesses. New rule #1 is you can pay as little as 10% down for business components. That's 60% less down payment to buy the same business. So, if you're paying $1,000,000 for a business, your down payment just changed from $250,000 to $100,000. You keep an extra $150,000 in cash while you're out buying cash flow.

Note that borrowers still must have the necessary collateral, credit score...etc., but these items have always been part of the equation. Banks (SBA lenders) have wasted no time jumping in with the revised terms. Remember, banking is a very competitive business and nobody wants to miss an opportunity.

New rule #2 is SBA lenders can allow seller financing for up to half of the 10% down payment as long as the seller financing piece is on full standby for the entire duration of the loan. Continuing with the example above and with the seller's agreement to finance half the down payment, the buyer would only need $50,000 in cash (collateral, credit score…) to buy a $1,000,000 business.

The Mechanics of Buying

Top Four Mistakes Buyers Make When Applying For Financing

Financing an early education company is sometimes the most difficult hurdle to clear whether you're acquiring childcare centers, preschools, Montessori schools or just refinancing your current debt. Hence, it's important to avoid any pitfalls that can make your borrowing process more difficult.

Here are four of the most common mistakes made when applying for a loan:

1. **Applying to only one lender.** Although there are many lenders who want to make good loans, people still tend to go to their local bank first without shopping around. While lenders are important, they are still vendors who can and should compete for your business. As the cost of financing is a material cost, you should always make sure of receiving the best terms to fit the project. Between banks and the SBA, there are many options that can help borrowers be more successful in their endeavors. It's always best to have multiple banks compete for your loan.

2. Not knowing if you demonstrate the ability to repay the loan. It is very normal to apply for a loan and not know if the bank (or other lender) will approve the loan. That's why we go through the lending process. However, and before you apply for a loan, it is a good idea to review your own cash flow internally so you know whether or not you feel you can repay the loan. Lenders will talk in terms of Debt Coverage Ratio or Debt Service Coverage. In English, they are simply checking to see if you have enough "cushion" to ensure that they get their money back when they lend it to you. Before you shop for financing, make sure you can report your income, expenses and profits (or losses) clearly. Be direct and honest with your lender. The faster a lender knows your correct numbers, the more quickly he or she can decide whether they can make the loan under terms that are acceptable to all parties.

3. Not knowing your credit rating. Every lender is going to need to know your credit score before they can do anything. Before you apply for a loan, you need to know your credit scores. If you are unsure of your credit score or think you might have blemishes on your credit report(s), it's best to get copies of the reports from the major credit reporting agencies. Having the reports in hand allows you, or you and your lender, to address any potential problems up front. You can contact the major credit reporting agencies via the Resources Page at www.bfsinc.net/ (BFS® receives no compensation for providing this access.).

4. Not having your finances up-to-date. Whether you are seeking a personal loan or a business loan, you will need to have your financial information in order for typically the last three complete years and the current year-to-date. Having this

information organized will help to expedite the borrowing process.

Lenders want to make good loans. The fewer questions they have to ask, the better the experience will be for you and your lender.

CLIENTS WORKING FROM BOTH SIDES

Occasionally, a client will work with us on both sides of separate transactions. For example, they will have us sell their center(s) in California so they can move back to North Carolina to take care of their aging parents. When someone has been on the selling or buying side of a transaction, it makes them better at the opposite side of a transaction the next time around.

CHAPTER FIFTY-THREE

How High Does My Credit Score Need To Be And How Do I Make It Better?

Here are a couple of general rules for your consideration. Your minimum credit score needs to be at least 650. A score of 700 or more is preferred. If your credit score is below 650 then there are ways to fix it. Here's how it works:

1. You can challenge anything in your credit report. If the merchant can't provide proof of their claim, then the item must be removed from your credit report. For example, if Department Store X says that you didn't pay off your $72 balance on your X card in 2015, and you say that you did, then Department Store X has 30 days to provide the documentation proving that the bill is unpaid. If they can't prove their claim, then the outstanding debt is removed and you're moving toward a higher credit score. If Department Store X is right and you do owe them $72, then you now know the problem and you have the opportunity to pay the $72…again you're moving toward a higher credit score.

2. Get and review copies of your three major credit reports annually–more often if you are nearing pivotal junctures where your credit score is especially important. Again, contact information for all three credit reporting agencies can be found on the Resources Page at www.bfsinc.net.

3. Between the reports from Federal Trade Commission ("FTC") and CBS News, it is estimated that somewhere between five and eighty percent of credit reports contain errors. Some errors are actually good for you and some are not so good. In my mid-twenties I checked my credit reports, and I was very happy to learn that not only had I purchased a new car, but I paid it off with a perfect history of payments. It was great for my young credit history—never did find the car.

4. Your credit score contains five components. Here are the five components and their degree of importance by percentage:

    a. Payment History (35%). Here, the credit bureaus (CBs) are looking at mortgages, credit cards, installment loans, retail accounts, adverse public records like bankruptcy, lawsuits, judgments, liens, garnishments, past due payments...etc. If you have past due payments, the CBs will look at (a) amount past due, (b) amount of time past due and (c) the number of accounts past due.

    b. Amounts Owed (30%). CBs are reviewing the type of accounts you use and the amount of credit you are utilizing relative to the credit available to you. For example and all else being equal, a person carrying balances equaling 95% of credit available on ten personal credit cards for a total of $50,000 outstanding debt will have a lower credit score than a person carrying 50% balances on three credit cards for a total of $10,000 outstanding debt.

c. **Length of Credit History (15%).** CBs are examining specific account types, how long the accounts have been open and the level and timing of activity within the account. Amazingly, for credit scoring purposes it appears that it is actually better to have credit accounts with outstanding balances (within reason) than to have no accounts open or no credit history. Being debt free can actually lower your credit score. I have a friend who is a very astute, very successful former international banker. He has done business in more than 20 countries and has lived in nine countries. This is a person with exceptional success, wealth, and highly responsible money management practices. He was turned down when he applied for a credit card at the very bank where he worked. Reason: No U.S. credit history.

d. **New Credit History (10%).** In short, the CBs are looking to see if you have been opening or attempting to open lots of new accounts recently. As you might imagine, someone who is thinking about lending you money gets very nervous when they discover you are borrowing money from everyone.

e. **Type of Credit Used (10%).** CBs look at the balance of debt as distributed throughout the various types of debt from credit cards to mortgages and secured to unsecured.

Your credit score is based on all of the items above. It is not a pass-fail circumstance for each of the categories. Your score is produced in the aggregate and that scoring constantly changes. The scoring for one person and their financial profile will be different from another person. The information presented here is for the fat part of the Bell Curve, but it provides solid guidelines.

If you are focused on an acquisition (or other type of loan) and your score is below the 650 mark, note that a business partner's score that is 700 or higher can help to offset your score. When lenders are considering borrower qualifications, they look at the entire "borrower" whether it is one person or a legion of people.

CHAPTER FIFTY-FOUR

What Information Should A Letter of Intent Include?

As it pertains to the buying and selling of centers and schools, a Letter of Intent ("LOI") is a written statement expressing the intention of the participating parties to enter into a formal agreement. A LOI is not a formal agreement or a binding contract although it can have binding parts. The LOI serves the very important purpose of defining the agreed upon terms of a transaction so there are no misunderstandings between the parties, but it does not provide the detail found in a Purchase Sale Agreement.

Letters of Intent vary in length and amount of detail; however, the goal is to provide enough detail so the major concerns are defined but not so much detail that the document borders on a purchase sale agreement. The following information is commonly found in a well-structured LOI:

1. Date of the LOI.

2. Names and Titles. This area should include the complete names of the buying, selling and brokerage companies and the individual signatories for each of these companies along with

their corporate titles…President, Secretary, Partner, Managing Member…etc.

3. Contact information for each of the companies and their representatives.

4. Asset (or stock) Identification. The LOI should identify the assets to be bought and sold in the transaction. For example: Assets of ABC Montessori, Inc. and real estate held in the name of XYZ, LLC and used in operations of ABC Montessori, Inc. Said assets and real estate are located at 123 Main Street, Any Town, Any State, 12345.

5. The Purchase Price.

6. Amount of buyer's good faith deposit and the company responsible for escrowing the deposit.

7. Terms of the transaction. Examples: All Cash at Closing…or $2,000,000 Cash and $250,000 Seller Financing.

8. Information pertaining to any lease to be entered into by the buyer. Example: Buyer and Seller agree to enter into a triple net lease with an original term of 10 years and three five-year options. Annual increases in the lease rate will be the lesser of CPI or 2.5% of prior year's rent. Again, the LOI is not drafting the lease. It is only establishing the primary terms.

9. Transaction Contingencies. Contingencies are items that would likely cause the buyer, seller or both to walk away from the transaction should there be a disagreement. For example:

    a. All Cash and Accounts receivable accrued up to the closing date will remain the property of the seller.

    b. Buyer's Good Faith Deposit will be refunded in full in the event buyer's due diligence reveals unacceptable conditions.

    c. Buyer's Good Faith Deposit will be refunded in full in the event buyer's financing is denied and written verification is submitted to XYZ Brokerage, Inc. on or before July 1, 20XX.

    d. Buyer will provide written verification of down payment funds in the amount of no less than $XXX,XXX upon signing of the LOI.

    e. Buyer and seller agree that seller is responsible for the payment of brokerage fees to XYZ Brokerage, Inc. in the amount of $XXX,XXX.

10. Closing Date. The Closing Date should be stated as On or Before…the Closing Date to provide flexibility to parties involved. Unless there are stated terms to the contrary or "timeline contingencies", it should also be stated the buyer and seller agree that the buyer has exclusive right to purchase said assets (or stock) up to and including the Closing Date.

11. Timeline Contingencies. These contingencies are the ones that keep a transaction moving forward at a timely pace. While nearly every transaction will have its challenges, it is important to closely watch the amount of time used for the various sub-processes like finishing the purchase sale agreement, securing financing, getting licensing approval, completing Phase One inspections, getting a real estate appraisal, having staff fingerprinted (in some states)...etc. A delay in one process can cause delays in other processes until a transaction stretches to nine months instead of the more normal four months. Some examples of timeline contingencies are as follows:

a. This LOI becomes invalid if it is not fully executed on or before X date.

b. Buyer agrees to provide first draft of purchase sale agreement on or before X date.

c. Buyer agrees to submit completed financing application to chosen lender on or before X date.

d. Buyer's lending institution will inform Seller of preliminary approval of Buyer's financing on or before X date.

e. Buyer's lending institution will inform Seller of final approval of Buyer's financing two weeks before Closing Date.

f. Seller agrees to notify state licensing of pending transaction within three days of receiving fully executed purchase sale agreement and notification of Buyer's receipt of Commitment Letter from Buyer's lender.

12. Include language that allows the LOI to be signed in counter-parts. Again, this is a small item but it can save you days in the process.

A Letter of Intent is a terrific tool for helping to get your transaction off to a good start and moving it toward closing more efficiently. While the information above certainly isn't exhaustive, it provides a great platform. Always consult the proper professional before acting.

CHAPTER FIFTY-FIVE

Funding Your Early Education Company

Many of us need money from other people to start and grow companies. The money comes from banks, partners, investors, venture capitalists, equity funds…and/or our closest friends and family. No matter what the source is, understand two things. One, there is always a cost to using someone else's money. Two, the cost can vary greatly between sources.

The first question is…Do I borrow money and go into debt or do I sell equity in my company to someone else? Keep in mind that equity is always more expensive than debt in a successful company. You only have to pay off debt one time. The payments on equity can last the entire life of your company. I have seen more than one person sell his or her company only to realize just how expensive equity can be. One example, my friend (a very smart guy) started his company and gave away a 20% equity stake in exchange for $50,000 of start-up capital. Over approximately 10 years, this 20% partner received 20% of all of the company profits and $5,200,000 when the company was sold. If he paid interest of 50% a year on the $50,000, his total repayment would have been $300,000.

When it comes to growing a successful early education company, responsible use of debt can be a great tool to expedite that growth. Here are some important things to consider when you're thinking about using debt:

1. Again, never accept a loan from any lender without having many lenders compete for your loan. No matter how you approach the process, competition amongst vendors is always in the best interest of the consumer.

2. When you see the loan that you think is right for you, do a detailed review (this means use a good attorney) to make sure there are no hidden fees or terms...no ambiguous language that can surprise you after you have already made the commitment. Some people think it's overkill, but it's not. Many banks and bankers (like car salesmen) take an approach that the paperwork is all just standard stuff...sign here...sign here. It's standard stuff because they're not the ones on the hook. Review the loan documents carefully.

3. Be transparent with your lender. There's nothing wrong with negotiating the best terms you can get, but don't hide anything. Be honest and be direct.

4. If you can, see how the lender works with their borrowers when things aren't going well. Everyone is friendly the day you sign the papers, but I have seen lenders become absolutely vicious toward early education company owners when they're getting tested. You want a lender that will work with you just in case everything doesn't go as planned.

CHAPTER FIFTY-SIX

How Can I Get The Best Loan Terms For My Early Education Company?

The answer is...don't just shop multiple banks, shop them aggressively and meticulously. If you're not the kind of person that wants to do that type of work, there are people who will do it for you and those people are far less expensive than the quarter-century mistake you can make by accepting the wrong loan.

Here's where you'll want to focus:

1. Collateral Requirements - amount, type and time to release.

    a. Amount - Banks, as they should, are always looking to have the most collateral they can secure. Many banks will simply ask for every major asset you have when they could approve your loan with less collateral. Scrutinize these requirements. Don't let it stand if you think you're giving up too much.

    b. Type - Banks like assets that are easily located, like real estate. That way if something goes wrong, they know exactly where to find it. Less attractive to banks are assets that are easily moved, like a car or gold coins. If you need, for example, $100,000 of collateral to secure a loan, don't tie up a $750,000 piece of property when you could use $100,000 worth of blue chip stock.

   c. Time To Release - Keep in mind that collateral is negotiable, not just in the amount or type of collateral you provide, but also in the amount of time the bank holds the collateral. Know that your collateral does not have to stay under the bank's hold for the duration of the loan. Assets used as loan collateral can be released before you repay the entire loan. Make sure you can breakout your collateral as soon as possible.

2. Interest Rate - This one is obvious, but know that bankers have a tendency to talk in terms of bigger rate moves such as discussing whether the rate will be 6% or 6.25%. Rates can be pinned in smaller increments. Instead of 6.25% or even 6.125%, a loan can be pegged to 6.057% (for example). On a $2,000,000 loan, that's $1,360 in the first year alone. It may not seem like much when you're looking at $2,000,000 (bankers know that), but you wouldn't put it in your paper shredder once a year.

3. Points – As I have said a few times, banking is a very competitive business. I can't remember when or if I have ever paid points on a loan...including the early days when we were young and broke. You should be able to find a bank that doesn't require points.

4. Pre-Payment Penalties - Depending on the type of loan you choose, starting with Conventional versus SBA, the norms for

penalty fee time frames are one, three or five years. As rates have been historically low in recent years, we tend not to worry about the refinancing component, but as we are discussing here, lower rates don't have to be the only reason for refinancing. If you can get materially better overall terms, then it's time to improve your position. If you're planning to pay off your loan early and simplify your balance sheet, then it's much better if you can get rid of this contingent liability as soon as possible. That means scrutinizing this factor before you accept the loan.

5. Paperwork - Organizing your documents for analysis by the banks' underwriters is a skill. Bankers want to make good loans. If your loan package is organized so that it fits into the "banker-speak" format, it makes it easier and faster for banks to say yes. Don't underestimate the value of speaking bank language fluently. It is a solid indicator that you are organized and savvy in the financing world, and organized and savvy leads to better terms.

6. Credit Score - Everyone would like to have an 800+ credit score, but that's not the case for most people. Some people have lower credit scores because they choose not to carry debt. There are many reasons for a less-than-perfect score. Be prepared to explain any blemishes on your credit record. Know what the bank sees before they see it. If you need to know more about improving or repairing your credit score, see https://bfsinc.net/high-credit-score-need/.

7. Type of Loan - Comparing both conventional loans and SBA loans is another way to improve the odds of getting the best loan for you.

8. **Protect Your Credit Score By Shopping Banks The Right Way** - Don't reduce your credit score by shopping banks the wrong way. When you're ready to shop banks or other lenders, time it so you're in front of the lenders during the same 30-day window. In the infinite wisdom of credit reporting, your credit score will typically drop about 8 points when you are shopping for financing. That's bad enough especially when you consider that a loan may very well make you a better credit risk—not worse. To add insult to injury, if you shop lenders over two different 30-day periods, for example March and April, you'll get hit for 8 points for each month. It's not a perfect science, but it's very close. Again, be organized and know the system.

9. **Confirm Bank's Track Record** - In an effort to keep their portfolios balanced, banks move into and out of industries. Ask your bank for confirmation that they have made/are making loans to early education companies.

10. **Ask for More** - Remember that banks are vendors. They are important and necessary vendors in most cases, but they are still vendors…and there are a lot of them. They work in an incredibly competitive environment. Don't be afraid to ask for more. Sometimes you'll get it.

CHAPTER FIFTY-SEVEN

What Are The Initial Questions I Should Ask About An Early Education Company If I'm Interested In Buying It?

The Initial Questions have only one goal. Determine whether a company is interesting to you or a waste of your time as quickly as possible. While the questions won't be exactly the same for everyone, the following should cover most, if not all, of your first look:

1. Location.

2. Annual Revenue.

3. Annual Cash Flow. Specifically, EBITDA and EBITDAR. It is important to closely define "cash flow" as many people have very loose definitions for this term. A misunderstanding here can cost you time and money.

4. Current appraised value of any real estate included in the deal.

5.   The original cost or current market value of any furniture, fixtures and equipment (FF&E) included in the transaction.

6.   The market value of the business component and how that market value was determined.

7.   The total asking price.

8.   Whether the company is properly licensed and in good standing with regulators.

You'll certainly have other questions, but these first few "qualifying" questions can save you time, energy and money when you're trying to identify the right candidate.

CHEAPER IS NOT BETTER

Our fees are very average, but of course everybody likes a bargain, and there's nothing wrong negotiating for a better price. Routinely, I will talk with people who will invariably say that one of our competitors will do the work cheaper. It's a very normal reaction as price is the initial and simplest way to compare services. I will explain our services and why they are priced very fairly and arguably low when compared to our results. Regardless, some people will always go for the less expensive option first. Depending on the service under discussion, many of the people who try the less expensive alternative will call us back anywhere from 60 days to a year later having learned that cheaper does not mean better. Service levels are not the same. Results are not the same. There's also a derivative of this issue when people hire a friend or someone they know locally or socially. I've made this same mistake in my own career. You hire someone largely because you have a higher comfort level with the person. This is one of those black or white things. Just because you go to church with someone or their cousin plays softball with your sister, does not make them good for the job - not to mention many personal relationships have been ruined by working together.

About BFS®

Brad Barnett is the Founder and President of BFS®. BFS® is the largest early education consulting and brokerage firm in the United States. BUT, it wasn't always that way. After graduating college with honors (the first person in his family to ever set foot on a college campus), Brad bought an $89 suit and at least once hopped a ride in the back of a pickup to get to his new job in investment banking. Brad Barnett set a precedent from the start...Do whatever it takes to keep your word.

After five years in investment banking and insurance, Brad started BFS®. Today, Brad and BFS® have more than 5,000 contacts spread through at least a half dozen countries, endorsements from early education professionals all over the U.S. and licensed professionals in 42 states and Washington, DC. For more (including lots of free resources), visit their website at www.bfsinc.net, go to the BFS® video library at www.bfsvideos.tv...or just call them at (800) 467-1774.

Summary of Services

SELLING YOUR EARLY EDUCATION COMPANY. Whether you want to sell your business, sell and lease your real estate or sell everything simultaneously, we are uniquely qualified to help you get the highest market value and best deal structure tailored to meet your requirements. Our selling clients receive all cash at closing as the BFS® network secures financing for buyers. All buyers are pre-qualified financially and educationally. BFS® systems ensure the absolute privacy and discretion necessary to sell your early education company safely. See more at www.bfsinc.net/selling and www.bfsinc.net/sale-and-leaseback

BUYING AN EARLY EDUCATION COMPANY. While BFS® never represents a buyer in the purchase of a BFS® selling client's company, BFS® teaches buyers to purchase early education companies safely and at prices that are materially lower than market value. We understand that you want to pay the lowest possible price for your acquisitions and that you definitely want to avoid making the wrong acquisition. We are perfectly positioned to ensure that you meet both goals. See more at www.bfsinc.net/buying.

FINANCING. BFS® vendors secure financing for people in the early education industry. We can have pre-approval of most loans within

72 hours of receipt of the preliminary application documents. Loans range from a minimum of $300,000 up to a maximum of $20,000,000 and can be used for any of the following:

• Business Acquisitions

• Purchase of Real Estate

• Mortgage Refinancing

• Renovation/Expansion of Facilities

• New Construction

• Sale and Leaseback of Real Estate

See more at www.bfsinc.net/financing

EVALUATING & IMPROVING.   BFS® provides very discreet, comprehensive evaluations of early education companies that include the business component market value, equipment market value and recommendations for improving profitability, operational efficiency and marketability. Our evaluations culminate in a detailed portfolio that should please the most discriminating reader. Because of BFS® discretion, your staff need not know the reason for our visit. Real estate appraisal is never included in a BFS® evaluation. See more at www.bfsinc.net/evaluations.   See additional free resources at www.bfsinc.net including (but not limited to) our Video Library, Instant Q & A, and Management Tips.

About The Author

Brad Barnett founded BFS® in 1993 after five years as an advisor in investment banking and insurance. Today, BFS® has licensed professionals in 42 states and Washington DC. Within the early education vertical, Brad is known for using his in-depth knowledge, directness and honesty to produce exceptional results. He has traveled the U.S. relentlessly over the last 25 years doing everything in the early education industry from saving early education companies from foreclosure and bankruptcy to leading their owners to multimillion dollar paydays. For more information, including information on the many free early education resources provided by BFS®, visit www.bfsinc.net.

If you are interested in having Brad speak to your organization or group, call (800) 467-1774.

www.ingramcontent.com/pod-product-compliance
Lightning Source LLC
Chambersburg PA
CBHW050527190326
41458CB00045B/6731/J